펴낸이	김기훈 · 김진희
펴낸곳	(주)쎄듀 / 서울시 강남구 논현로 305 (역삼동)
발행일	2018년 9월 14일 제1개정판 1쇄
내용문의	www.cedubook.com
구입문의	콘텐츠 마케팅 사업본부
	Tel. 02-6241-2007
	Fax. 02-2058-0209
등록번호	제 22-2472호
ISBN	978-89-6806-126-4

저자

쎄듀 영어교육연구센터
쎄듀 영어교육센터는 영어 콘텐츠에 대한 전문지식과 경험을 바탕으로
최고의 교육 콘텐츠를 만들고자 최선의 노력을 다하는 전문가 집단입니다.
조현미 선임연구원 · **최세림** 전임연구원

기획	푸른나무교육(GTE) Korea
마케팅	콘텐츠 마케팅 사업본부
영업	문병구
제작	정승호
인디자인 편집	푸른나무교육(GTE) Korea
디자인	윤혜영
영문교열	Adam Miller

READING 16

LEVEL. 3

OVERVIEW 이 책의 구성

➡ 유형 소개 & 유형 전략

문제 유형별 특징 소개 & 문제 해결 전략 제시

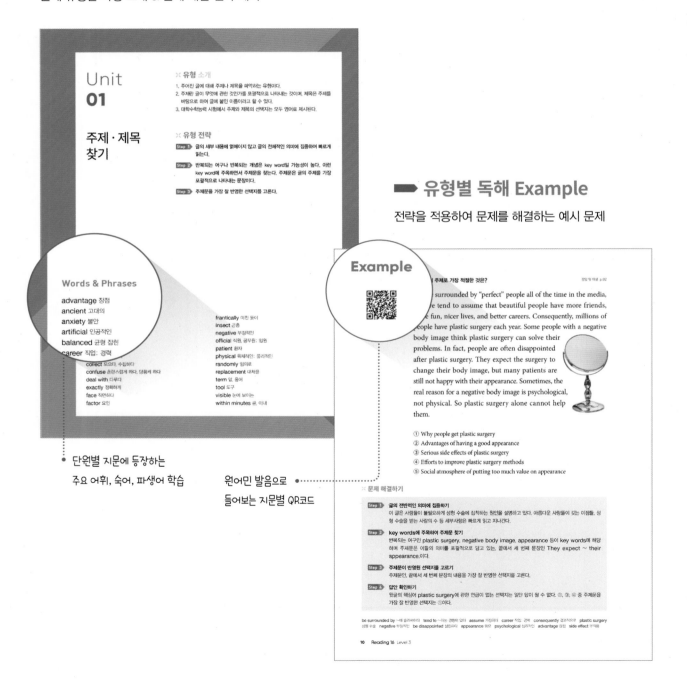

Unit 01

주제·제목 찾기

Words & Phrases

advantage 장점
ancient 고대의
anxiety 불안
artificial 인공적인
balanced 균형 잡힌
career 직업; 경력

collect 모으다, 수집하다
confuse 혼란스럽게 하다, 당황하게 하다
deal with 다루다
exactly 정확하게
face 직면하다
factor 요인

※ 유형 소개
1. 주어진 글에 대해 주제나 제목을 파악하는 유형이다.
2. 주제란 글이 무엇에 관한 것인가를 포괄적으로 나타내는 것이며, 제목은 주제를 바탕으로 하여 글에 붙인 이름이라고 할 수 있다.
3. 대학수학능력 시험에서 주제와 제목의 선택지는 모두 영어로 제시된다.

※ 유형 전략
Step 1 글의 세부 내용에 얽매이지 않고 글의 전체적인 의미에 집중하여 빠르게 읽는다.
Step 2 반복되는 어구나 반복되는 개념은 key word일 가능성이 높다. 이런 key word에 주목하면서 주제문을 찾는다. 주제문은 글의 주제를 가장 포괄적으로 나타내는 문장이다.
Step 3 주제문을 가장 잘 반영한 선택지를 고른다.

frantically 미친 듯이
insect 곤충
negative 부정적인
official 직원, 공무원; 임원
patient 환자
physical 육체적인; 물리적인
randomly 임의로
replacement 대체물
term 말, 용어
tool 도구
visible 눈에 보이는
within minutes 곧, 이내

• 단원별 지문에 등장하는
주요 어휘, 숙어, 파생어 학습

원어민 발음으로
들어보는 지문별 QR코드

➡ 유형별 독해 Example

전략을 적용하여 문제를 해결하는 예시 문제

Example

정답 및 해설 p.02

글의 주제로 가장 적절한 것은?

surrounded by "perfect" people all of the time in the media, tend to assume that beautiful people have more friends, fun, nicer lives, and better careers. Consequently, millions of people have plastic surgery each year. Some people with a negative body image think plastic surgery can solve their problems. In fact, people are often disappointed after plastic surgery. They expect the surgery to change their body image, but many patients are still not happy with their appearance. Sometimes, the real reason for a negative body image is psychological, not physical. So plastic surgery alone cannot help them.

① Why people get plastic surgery
② Advantages of having a good appearance
③ Serious side effects of plastic surgery
④ Efforts to improve plastic surgery methods
⑤ Social atmosphere of putting too much value on appearance

문제 해결하기

Step 1 글의 전반적인 의미에 집중하기
이 글은 사람들이 불필요하게 성형 수술에 집착하는 원인을 설명하고 있다. 아름다운 사람들이 갖는 이점들, 성형 수술을 받는 사람의 수 등 세부사항은 빠르게 읽고 지나간다.

Step 2 key words에 주목하여 주제문 찾기
반복되는 어구인 plastic surgery, negative body image, appearance 등이 key words에 해당하며 주제문은 이들의 의미를 포괄적으로 담고 있는, 끝에서 세 번째 문장인 They expect ~ their appearance.이다.

Step 3 주제문이 반영된 선택지 고르기
주제문인, 끝에서 세 번째 문장의 내용을 가장 잘 반영한 선택지를 고른다.

Step 4 답안 확인하기
윗글의 핵심어 plastic surgery에 관한 언급이 없는 선택지는 일단 답이 될 수 없다. ①, ③, ④ 중 주제문을 가장 잘 반영한 선택지는 ①이다.

be surrounded by ~에 둘러싸이다 tend to ~하는 경향이 있다 assume 가정하다 career 직업; 경력 consequently 결과적으로 plastic surgery 성형 수술 negative 부정적인 be disappointed 실망하다 appearance 외모 psychological 심리적인 advantage 장점 side effect 부작용

➡ 유형별 독해 Practice

실전 연습을 위한 다양한 소재의 독해 지문 + 심화 학습을 위한 장문 독해

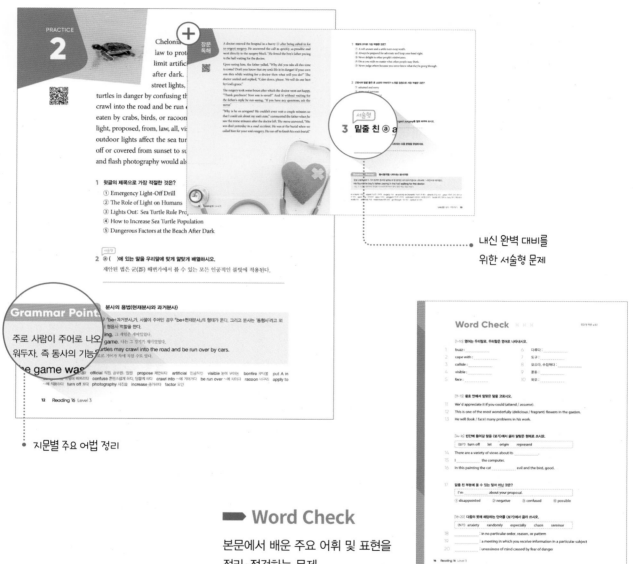

내신 완벽 대비를
위한 서술형 문제

지문별 주요 어법 정리

➡ Word Check

본문에서 배운 주요 어휘 및 표현을
정리·점검하는 문제

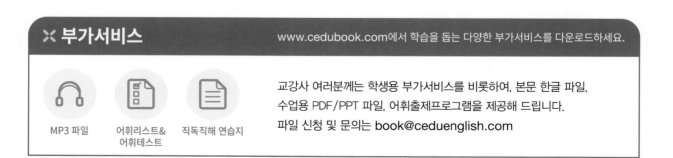

CONTENTS 목차

Unit 01

주제·제목 찾기

✕ 유형 소개

1. 주어진 글에 대해 주제나 제목을 파악하는 유형이다.
2. 주제란 글이 무엇에 관한 것인가를 포괄적으로 나타내는 것이며, 제목은 주제를 바탕으로 하여 글에 붙인 이름이라고 할 수 있다.
3. 대학수학능력 시험에서 주제와 제목의 선택지는 모두 영어로 제시된다.

✕ 유형 전략

Step 1 글의 세부 내용에 얽매이지 않고 글의 전체적인 의미에 집중하여 빠르게 읽는다.

Step 2 반복되는 어구나 반복되는 개념은 key word일 가능성이 높다. 이런 key word에 주목하면서 주제문을 찾는다. 주제문은 글의 주제를 가장 포괄적으로 나타내는 문장이다.

Step 3 주제문을 가장 잘 반영한 선택지를 고른다.

Words & Phrases

advantage 장점
ancient 고대의
anxiety 불안
artificial 인공적인
balanced 균형 잡힌
career 직업; 경력
collect 모으다, 수집하다
confuse 혼란스럽게 하다, 당황케 하다
deal with 다루다
exactly 정확하게
face 직면하다
factor 요인

frantically 미친 듯이
insect 곤충
negative 부정적인
official 직원, 공무원; 임원
patient 환자
physical 육체적인; 물리적인
randomly 임의로
replacement 대체물
term 말, 용어
tool 도구
visible 눈에 보이는
within minutes 곧, 이내

Example

다음 글의 주제로 가장 적절한 것은?

정답 및 해설 p.02

We are surrounded by "perfect" people all of the time in the media, and we tend to assume that beautiful people have more friends, more fun, nicer lives, and better careers. Consequently, millions of people have plastic surgery each year. Some people with a negative body image think plastic surgery can solve their problems. In fact, people are often disappointed after plastic surgery. They expect the surgery to change their body image, but many patients are still not happy with their appearance. Sometimes, the real reason for a negative body image is psychological, not physical. So plastic surgery alone cannot help them.

① Why people get plastic surgery
② Advantages of having a good appearance
③ Serious side effects of plastic surgery
④ Efforts to improve plastic surgery methods
⑤ Social atmosphere of putting too much value on appearance

✖ 문제 해결하기

Step 1 글의 전반적인 의미에 집중하기
이 글은 사람들이 불필요하게 성형 수술에 집착하는 원인을 설명하고 있다. 아름다운 사람들이 갖는 이점들, 성형 수술을 받는 사람의 수 등 세부사항은 빠르게 읽고 지나간다.

Step 2 key words에 주목하여 주제문 찾기
반복되는 어구인 plastic surgery, negative body image, appearance 등이 key words에 해당하며 주제문은 이들의 의미를 포괄적으로 담고 있는, 끝에서 세 번째 문장인 They expect ~ their appearance.이다.

Step 3 주제문이 반영된 선택지를 고르기
주제문인, 끝에서 세 번째 문장의 내용을 가장 잘 반영한 선택지를 고른다.

Step 4 답안 확인하기
윗글의 핵심어 plastic surgery에 관한 언급이 없는 선택지는 일단 답이 될 수 없다. ①, ③, ④ 중 주제문을 가장 잘 반영한 선택지는 ①이다.

be surrounded by ~에 둘러싸이다 tend to ~하는 경향이 있다 assume 가정하다 career 직업; 경력 consequently 결과적으로 plastic surgery 성형 수술 negative 부정적인 be disappointed 실망하다 appearance 외모 psychological 심리적인 advantage 장점 side effect 부작용

Work. Money. Anxiety. Sickness. *Did you feel your stress level rise as you read those words? These terms represent some of the more difficult things that we face every day in life. Sunshine. Autumn leaves. Falling water. Fragrant flowers. Did you feel yourself start to relax that time? Is the buzz in your head slowing down? It's amazing that simply imagining the elements of a garden can quickly improve our mood and give us the strength to deal with the difficult things in our day. Gardens have been used as a tool for healing for centuries. For everything from ancient herbal remedies to modern-day health and rest at home, we have looked to nature to help us heal. Today, the garden is again becoming an important part of the way we live and cope with our busy lives.

1 윗글의 제목으로 가장 적절한 것은?

① The Origin of the Garden
② The Healing Power of Gardens
③ The Relationship Between Nature and Humans
④ Common Elements of a Garden
⑤ People's Health Problems Caused by Stress

서술형
2 다음 문장을 주어진 어구로 시작하는 문장으로 바꾸어 쓰시오.

The elements of a garden can quickly improve our mood.

→ Our mood can _____.

Grammar Points!　**지각동사의 목적격 보어**

지각동사(smell, hear, see, feel 등)의 목적격 보어로는 동사원형을 취하며, '(주어)는 (목적어)가 (목적격 보어)하는 것을 (지각동사)한다' 로 해석한다.

Did you feel your stress level rise as you read those words?
당신은 이러한 낱말을 읽을 때 스트레스 정도가 올라가는 것을 느꼈는가?

---

term 말, 용어　**represent** 나타내다　**face** 직면하다　**fragrant** 향기로운 (*n.* fragrance 향기)　**buzz** 소란스런 소리　**slow down** 느긋해지다　**ancient** 고대의　**herbal remedy** 약초 요법　**look to** ~에 의지하다　**cope with** ~에 대처하다　**origin** 기원　**relationship** 관계

Chelonia County officials have proposed a new law to protect baby sea turtles. The law would limit artificial light that is visible from beaches after dark. Artificial light, such as light from street lights, house lights, or bonfires, can put sea turtles in danger by confusing them. *Confused baby sea turtles may crawl into the road and be run over by cars. The turtles may also be eaten by crabs, birds, or racoons. ⓐ (county beaches, the, artificial lights, proposed, from, law, all, visible, applies to). As both indoor and outdoor lights affect the sea turtles, lights would have to be turned off or covered from sunset to sunrise. In addition, bright flashlights and flash photography would also not be allowed.

1 윗글의 제목으로 가장 적절한 것은?

① Emergency Light-Off Drill
② The Role of Light on Humans
③ Lights Out: Sea Turtle Rule Proposed
④ How to Increase Sea Turtle Population
⑤ Dangerous Factors at the Beach After Dark

서술형

2 ⓐ ( )에 있는 말을 우리말에 맞게 알맞게 배열하시오.

제안된 법은 군(郡) 해변가에서 볼 수 있는 모든 인공적인 불빛에 적용된다.

Grammar Points! 분사의 용법(현재분사와 과거분사)

주로 사람이 주어로 나오는 경우 『be+과거분사』가, 사물이 주어인 경우 『be+현재분사』의 형태가 온다. 그리고 분사는 '동형사'라고 외워두자. 즉 동사의 기능을 하면서 형용사 역할을 한다.
The game **was interesting**. 그 게임은 재미있었다.
I **was interested** in the game. 나는 그 경기가 재미있었다.
Confused baby sea turtles may crawl into the road and be run over by cars.
당황한 아기 바다거북들은 도로로 기어가 차에 치일 수도 있다.

county (행정구역상) 군(郡) official 직원, 공무원; 임원 propose 제안하다 artificial 인공적인 visible 눈에 보이는 bonfire 모닥불 put A in danger A를 위험에 빠뜨리다 confuse 혼란스럽게 하다. 당황케 하다 crawl into ~에 기어가다 be run over ~에 치이다 racoon 너구리 apply to ~에 적용하다 turn off 끄다 photography 사진술 increase 증가하다 factor 요인

Gabriela Casas, a researcher at the Institute of Ecology at the National Autonomous University of Mexico(UNAM) says that some insects and their eggs are nutritionally beneficial to (A) these / those who suffer from diabetes. Ten years ago, when she was diagnosed with the disease herself, she tried to find a way to achieve a more balanced, sugar-free diet. In her research, she found that many insects had high levels of protein and amino acids. When they are dried and (B) grind / ground up, the insect powder can be used as a replacement for wheat flour. The switch to an insect diet has helped keep her condition under control. Casas also says consuming insects can be helpful to the environment. Now, as a part of her job, Casas gives educational talks about the advantages of eating insects. *She says children are easier to convince than their parents, (C) that / which is a good sign for the future.

1 윗글의 주제로 가장 적절한 것은?

① the many nutrients in insects ② the benefits of eating insects
③ the side effects of eating insects ④ the effective ways to cure diabetes
⑤ the appearance of a new insect diet

서술형
2 (A), (B), (C)에서 어법에 맞는 것을 골라 쓰시오.

(A) _____ (B) _____ (C) _____

Grammar Points! **능동태 vs. 수동태**

주어가 동사의 동작을 행하는 상황을 나타낼 때는 능동태가, 주어가 동사의 동작을 받는 상황을 나타낼 때는 수동태가 온다.
When **they are** dried and **ground** up, the insect powder can be used as a replacement for
= many insects

wheat flour.
그것들(많은 곤충들)이 말리거나 완전히 갈렸을 때, 그 곤충가루는 밀가루 대체물로써 사용될 수 있다.

---

researcher 연구가 institute 학회, 연구소 ecology 생태학 autonomous 자치의, 자치권이 있는 insect 곤충 nutritionally 영양학적으로 suffer from ~로 고통을 겪다 diabetes 당뇨병 be diagnosed with ~로 진단받다 balanced 균형 잡힌 sugar-free 무설탕의 protein 단백질 grind up ~을 (완전히) 갈다 replacement 대체물 switch to ~로의 전환[바꿈] advantage 이점 convince 설득시키다. 납득시키다

Once, a group of fifty people were attending a seminar. Suddenly, the speaker stopped and decided to do a group activity. He started giving each person a balloon. The group was asked to write their names on their balloons using a marker pen. Then all the balloons were collected and put in another room. Afterward, the people were let in the other room and given five minutes to find the balloon that had their name written on it. Everyone frantically searched for their balloon. They collided with one another and pushed others out of the way; it was complete chaos. At the end of the five minutes, no one had found their own balloon. Then the group was asked to randomly collect a balloon and give it to the person whose name was written on it. Within minutes, everyone had their own balloon. The speaker began: Exactly <u>this</u> is happening in our lives. *Everyone is frantically looking for happiness all around, not knowing where it is. Our happiness lies in the happiness of other people. Give them their happiness, and you will get _____.

1 윗글의 제목으로 가장 적절한 것은?

① How Can We Be Happy?
② Never Miss Balloons for Your Party!
③ Teamwork Is Always the Best Policy
④ True Happiness Is in Your Mind
⑤ Happiness Is Like a Fun Game

2 윗글의 빈칸에 들어갈 말로 가장 적절한 것은?

① the balloons
② their praise
③ success in your life
④ your own happiness
⑤ true love as a reward

3 밑줄 친 this가 가리키는 내용으로 알맞은 것은?

① 쾌락을 추구하는 것
② 물질적 부만 추구하는 것
③ 잘못된 방법으로 행복을 찾는 것
④ 본의 아니게 타인을 곤경에 빠뜨리는 것
⑤ 행복은 항상 멀리 있다고 생각하는 것

서술형

4 balloon이 상징하는 것을 윗글에서 찾아 한 단어로 나타내시오.

_____

Grammar Points! 　분사구문의 부정 의미

분사구문을 부정할 때 부정어 not은 분사 바로 앞에 위치한다.
Everyone is frantically looking for happiness all around, <u>not</u> knowing where it is.
　　　　　　　　　　　　　　　　　　　　　　　= as they don't know
사람들은 모두 행복이 어디에 있는지 모른 채 미친 듯이 사방에서 행복을 찾는다.

attend 참석하다　seminar 세미나　afterward 그 후에　let 하게 하다　frantically 미친 듯이　collide 충돌하다　push ~ out of the way ～을 밀어
내다　complete 완벽한, 완전한　chaos 혼돈　within minutes 곧, 이내

Word Check ✕ ✕ ✕

정답 및 해설 p.03

[1-10] 영어는 우리말로, 우리말은 영어로 나타내시오.

1 buzz : _____

2 cope with : _____

3 collide : _____

4 visible : _____

5 face : _____

6 다루다 : _____

7 도구 : _____

8 모으다, 수집하다 : _____

9 혼돈 : _____

10 외모 : _____

[11-13] 괄호 안에서 알맞은 말을 고르시오.

11 We'd appreciate it if you could (attend / assume).

12 This is one of the most wonderfully (delicious / fragrant) flowers in the garden.

13 He will (look / face) many problems in his work.

[14-16] 빈칸에 들어갈 말을 〈보기〉에서 골라 알맞은 형태로 쓰시오.

〈보기〉 turn off   let   origin   represent

14 There are a variety of views about its _____.

15 I _____ the computer.

16 In this painting the cat _____ evil and the bird, good.

17 밑줄 친 부분에 올 수 있는 말이 <u>아닌</u> 것은?

I'm _____ about your proposal.

① disappointed   ② negative   ③ confused   ④ possible

[18-20] 다음의 뜻에 해당하는 단어를 〈보기〉에서 골라 쓰시오.

〈보기〉 anxiety   randomly   especially   chaos   seminar

18 _____ : in no particular order, reason, or pattern

19 _____ : a meeting in which you receive information in a particular subject

20 _____ : uneasiness of mind caused by fear of danger

Unit 02

요지·주장 찾기

✕ 유형 소개

1. 필자가 말하고자 하는 중심 내용인 요지나 주장을 파악하는 유형이다.
2. 정보를 소개하고 사실을 설명하는 설명문과 주장을 펼치는 논설문 지문에 자주 출제되는 유형이다.
3. 글의 전개 방식을 빠르게 파악하고 글에서 전달하고자 하는 핵심 내용과 세부 사항을 구별하여 판단할 수 있는 능력이 필요하다.
4. 요지를 담고 있는 핵심 문장이 단락 안에 명백히 드러나 있는 경우가 대부분이지만 글 전체에 언급된 내용을 종합하여 요지를 추론해내야 하는 경우도 종종 있다.

✕ 유형 전략

Step 1 글의 도입부와 마지막 부분을 읽고 서술 내용의 중심인 주제를 파악한다.

Step 2 요지나 주장을 직접적으로 드러내기 전에 상반된 견해를 먼저 언급하는 경우가 많으므로 대조의 연결사(but, however) 뒤에 오는 내용에 주목한다. 요지나 주장을 드러내는 표현(의무 조동사, 강조, 비교 표현 등)을 담고 있는 문장에도 주의한다.

Step 3 자주 등장하는 글의 전개 방식을 파악해 두면 요지 및 주장을 빠르게 파악할 수 있다. (중심 내용과 세부사항 열거, 비교와 대조, 원인과 결과, 문제 제기와 해결 방안 제시, 통념과 이에 대한 반론 등)

Words & Phrases

achievement 성취
advertise 광고하다
attitude 자세, 태도
be curious about ～에 호기심을 갖다
calm down 진정하다
claim 주장; 주장하다
comment 비평하다, 의견을 말하다
control 통제하다, 지배하다
decline 쇠퇴하다
directly 곧장, 바로
essential 필수적인
exist 존재하다 (n. existence 존재)
gradually 점차

isolated 고립된
misfortune 불행, 불운
neglected 소홀히 했던
overrate 과대평가하다
pace 천천히 걷다, 왔다 갔다 하다
popular 대중적인
prefer 선호하다
promote 증진시키다, 장려하다
save 구하다
structure 구조, 체계
sympathy 동정, 연민
technology 기술
urgent 다급한, 긴박한

Example

다음 글의 요지로 가장 적절한 것은?

정답 및 해설 p.03

In the olden days, schools educated students on every aspect of life. Students used to stay at their teacher's place and received education on various disciplines. However, as social structures changed, education became more and more job oriented, and attention to moral ethics gradually declined. Even though attention has always been placed on the development of people's best characteristics, such as honesty, sympathy, love, and compassion, more and more emphasis is now placed on materialistic achievements. Individuals do not care much about honesty and truth, but they feel pride for their worldly possessions like a good and big house or an expensive car. This change in society's attitude now affects both family relations and social relations. Younger generations can even be seen arguing with their elders, which was an almost nonexistent circumstance years ago.

① 현대의 교육은 윤리 교육을 간과하고 직업 교육에 중점을 둔다.
② 생활 전반에 대한 교육이 이루어졌던 과거를 본받아야 한다.
③ 사회가 변하면 교육의 방식도 바뀔 수밖에 없다.
④ 요즘 교육은 도덕적 가치보다는 물질적 성취를 더 강조한다.
⑤ 윤리 교육의 약화로 신구 세대의 갈등이 커지고 있다.

✕ 문제 해결하기

Step 1 처음 한두 문장 뒤에 나오는 대조의 연결사(but, however)에 주목하기
이 글의 첫 두 문장은 생활 전반에 걸쳐 교육이 이루어진 과거를 언급하고 있다. 그런 다음 대조의 연결사 However 뒤부터는 직업 교육이 강조되는 현재의 교육을 설명하고 있다. 본론에서 말하고자 하는 바를 효과적으로 전달하고자 대조의 방식을 취하고 있다.

Step 2 요지를 담고 있는 문장 찾기
글의 요지는 단락의 처음이나 끝 한두 문장에 드러나 있는 경우가 많지만, 이 글에서처럼 단락 중간 부분에 드러나 있는 경우도 있다. However로 시작하는 문장이 이 글의 요지 문장이고 이후 문장들은 이를 보충 설명하고 있다.

Step 3 요지를 잘 표현하고 있는 선택지 고르기
글에서 말하고자 하는 내용보다 지나치게 넓거나(general) 좁은(specific) 의미를 담고 있는 선택지를 답으로 택하지 않도록 주의해야 한다.

aspect 측면 various 다양한 discipline 훈련; (학문) 분야 structure 구조, 체계 oriented 지향의, 중심의 attention 관심 ethics 윤리학, 윤리 gradually 점차 decline 쇠퇴하다 sympathy 동정, 연민 emphasis 강조 materialistic 물질(만능)주의적인 achievement 성취 individual 개인 possession 소유 (pl. 재산) circumstance 상황

Today, the computer is king. Computers are in our cars, homes, offices — everywhere. Technology controls our lives. We have machines that do everything for us, from washing our clothes to making our food. *Many people think this is wonderful. They like the comfort of modern living. According to a survey, however, 70 percent of Americans think that technology makes people lazier. *Sixty-five percent think that it makes people more isolated. Perhaps <u>this</u> explains why some people dislike society's dependency on modern technology. They prefer the simple life of the past. They want to live without modern technology.

1 윗글의 요지로 가장 적절한 것은?

① Computers have revolutionized people's lifestyle.
② We can't live without modern conveniences.
③ The importance of modern technology can't be overestimated.
④ Most people are aware of the negative aspects of technology.
⑤ Lots of people try not to go back to the simple life of the past.

서술형

2 밑줄 친 this가 가리키는 내용을 우리말로 쓰시오.

_____

Grammar Points! 명사절을 이끄는 접속사 that

접속사 that이 이끄는 명사절은 문장에서 주어, 목적어, 보어 역할을 한다. 목적어로 쓰이는 경우, that은 생략할 수 있다.
Many people think **(that)** this is wonderful. 많은 사람은 이것이 멋지다고 생각한다.
　　　　　　　　　 (목적어)
Sixty-five percent think **that it makes people more isolated.** 65%는 그것이 사람들을 더욱 고립시킨다고 생각한다.
　　　　　　　　　　　　 (목적어)

technology 기술　control 통제하다, 지배하다　comfort 편안함, 안락　according to ~에 따르면　survey 조사　isolated 고립된　dependency 의존　prefer 선호하다　revolutionize 혁신을 일으키다　convenience 편의, 편리; 편의 시설　overestimate 과대평가하다

Vacations are overrated – or at least the way most people spend them. After working hard all year, *they spend all their money to make themselves exhausted during their vacation. Instead of taking a package tour of some exotic land, visiting five countries in six days and ⓐ (take) photographs of being in front of some famous places, why don't they just stay at home and relax? They could read the book that they've always been curious about. They could work on a neglected hobby. They could spend some quality time with their family and make their relationships closer. Then when they go back to work, they would feel energized and happy again.

1 윗글에서 필자가 주장하는 바로 가장 적절한 것은?

① 초보자에게는 패키지여행이 수월하다.

② 일정에 얽매이지 않는 여행을 위해서는 자유여행이 좋다.

③ 여행에서 남는 것은 사진이므로 많이 찍어두는 것이 좋다.

④ 여행은 우리들의 자신을 되돌아볼 수 있는 시간을 제공해준다.

⑤ 휴가 때 여행보다는 가정에서 양질의 시간을 보내는 것이 더 효율적이다.

> 서술형

2 ⓐ (take)의 동사를 어법에 맞게 알맞게 변형하시오.

_____

> **Grammar Points!** make + 목적어 + 목적격 보어[과거분사]
>
> 목적어와 목적격 보어와의 관계가 수동일 경우 목적격 보어로 '과거분사'를 쓴다.
> They spend all their money to **make themselves exhausted** during their vacation.
> 그들은 휴가 동안에 자신이 녹초가 되면서까지 모든 돈을 쓴다.
> I can't **make myself understood** in English. 나는 영어로 의사소통할 수 없다.

overrate 과대평가하다 at least 적어도 spend 보내다. 소비하다 take a package tour of ~의 패키지여행을 하다 exotic 이국적인 take photographs of ~의 사진을 찍다 be curious about ~에 호기심을 갖다 neglected 소홀히 했던 quality time 좋은 시간 energized 활기찬

*You have been told that you should drink a cup of milk every day for your health. They say milk is a "perfect food," as it has essential nutrients for our body. It is believed that calcium and other vitamins and minerals in milk make it an important part of a healthful diet for people of all ages. However, some scientific studies have found that, contrary to popular belief, drinking milk may do more harm to our bodies than good. Interestingly, milk can contribute to obesity, calcium deficiency, allergies, heart disease, cancer, and other health ailments. Opponents of drinking milk argue that claims regarding milk's benefits are merely advertising campaigns designed to promote dairy sales. They think that many nutritious alternatives to cow's milk exist.

1 윗글의 요지로 가장 적절한 것은?

① Milk is a perfect food that we have to drink every day.
② It is a misconception that milk is a perfect food.
③ Milk has lots of benefits, but it can be harmful to certain types of people.
④ Drinking too much milk can cause some kinds of diseases.
⑤ Consumers should be aware of deception in advertisements.

[서술형]

2 우유 반대론자들은 우유가 이롭다는 주장에 대해 어떻게 생각하고 있는지 우리말로 쓰시오.

_____

Grammar Points! 현재완료 수동태

과거부터 현재에 이르기까지의 시간을 이야기함과 동시에 주어가 동사의 동작을 받는 상황을 나타낼 때
「S + have been + p.p.(과거분사)」의 형태로 나타낸다.
You **have been told** that you should drink a cup of milk every day for your health.
당신은 건강을 위해 매일 우유 한 잔을 마셔야 한다는 말을 들어왔다.

essential 필수적인   nutrient 영양소   mineral 무기물   contrary to ~와 반대로   popular 대중적인   contribute ~의 원인이 되다. 기여하다(to)
obesity 비만   ailment 병; 불쾌   opponent 적, 반대자 (v. oppose 반대하다)   claim 주장; 주장하다   regarding ~에 관한   benefit 이점, 혜택
advertise 광고하다   designed 계획된   promote 증진시키다. 장려하다   exist 존재하다 (n. existence 존재)   misconception 오해, 잘못된 생각

A doctor entered the hospital in a hurry ⓐ after being called in for an urgent surgery. He answered the call as quickly as possible and went directly to the surgery block. *He found the boy's father pacing in the hall waiting for the doctor.

Upon seeing him, the father yelled, "Why did you take all this time to come? Don't you know that my son's life is in danger? If your own son dies while waiting for a doctor then what will you do?" The doctor smiled and replied, "Calm down, please. We will do our best by God's grace."

The surgery took some hours after which the doctor went out happy, "Thank goodness! Your son is saved!" And ⓑ without waiting for the father's reply he ran saying, "If you have any questions, ask the nurse."

"Why is he so arrogant? He couldn't even wait a couple minutes so that I could ask about my son's state," commented the father when he saw the nurse minutes after the doctor left. The nurse answered, "His son died yesterday in a road accident. He was at the burial when we called him for your son's surgery. He ran off to finish his son's burial."

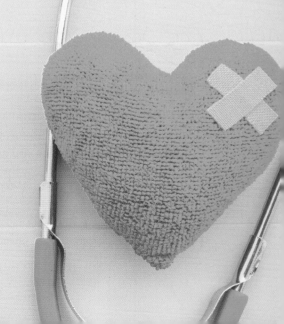

1 윗글의 요지로 가장 적절한 것은?

① A soft answer and a smile turn away wrath.

② Always be prepared for adversity and keep your head right.

③ Never delight in other people's misfortunes.

④ Do as you wish no matter what other people may think.

⑤ Never judge others because you never know what they're going through.

2 간호사의 말을 들은 후 소년의 아버지가 느꼈을 감정으로 가장 적절한 것은?

① ashamed and sorry

② angry and nervous

③ relieved and thankful

④ shocked and frightened

⑤ doubtful and cynical

[서술형]

3 밑줄 친 ⓐ after being called in for an urgent surgery를 절로 바꾸어 쓰시오.

_____

[서술형]

4 의사가 밑줄 친 ⓑ와 같이 행동한 이유를 나타내는 다음 문장을 완성하시오.

It was because he had to _____.

Grammar Points!　　동시동작을 나타내는 분사구문

동일 인물에 대해 두 가지 동작이 동시에 일어날 때 한 동작은 대개 분사구문으로 나타내며, '~하면서'로 해석한다.
He found the boy's father pacing in the hall waiting for the doctor.
그는 그 소년의 아버지가 의사를 기다리며 복도에서 왔다 갔다 하는 것을 보았다.

in a hurry 서둘러　urgent 다급한, 긴박한　surgery 수술　as quickly as possible 가능한 한 빨리　directly 곧장, 바로　pace 천천히 걷다, 왔다 갔다 하다　upon -ing ~하자마자　save 구하다　arrogant 거만한, 오만한　comment 비평하다, 의견을 말하다　burial 매장, 장례 (v. bury 묻다, 매장하다)　wrath 분노　adversity 역경　misfortune 불행, 불운　go through ~을 겪다　cynical 냉소적인

Word Check ✕ ✕ ✕

정답 및 해설 p.05

[1-10] 영어는 우리말로, 우리말은 영어로 나타내시오.

1 comfort : ＿＿＿＿＿＿＿＿＿＿

2 obesity : ＿＿＿＿＿＿＿＿＿＿

3 aspect : ＿＿＿＿＿＿＿＿＿＿

4 ethics : ＿＿＿＿＿＿＿＿＿＿

5 burial : ＿＿＿＿＿＿＿＿＿＿

6 영양소 : ＿＿＿＿＿＿＿＿＿＿

7 대안, 양자택일 : ＿＿＿＿＿＿＿＿＿＿

8 거만한, 오만한 : ＿＿＿＿＿＿＿＿＿＿

9 다급한, 긴박한 : ＿＿＿＿＿＿＿＿＿＿

10 존재하다 : ＿＿＿＿＿＿＿＿＿＿

[11-13] 괄호 안에서 알맞은 말을 고르시오.

11 She modeled to (provide / promote) the company's products.

12 There are many risk factors that (comment / contribute) to heart attacks.

13 The man (claimed / proposed) that he was a relative.

[14-16] 빈칸에 들어갈 말을 〈보기〉에서 골라 알맞은 형태로 쓰시오.

〈보기〉 campaign   design   prefer

14 The process is ＿＿＿＿＿＿＿＿＿ to be environmentally friendly.

15 I ＿＿＿＿＿＿＿＿＿ working with people to working alone.

16 The ＿＿＿＿＿＿＿＿＿ has encouraged teenagers to develop productive habits.

17 **두 단어의 관계가 나머지 넷과 다른 하나를 고르시오.**

① diligent – lazy   ② absent – present   ③ do good – do harm

④ classic – modern   ⑤ deficiency – lack

[18-20] 다음의 뜻에 해당하는 단어를 〈보기〉에서 골라 쓰시오.

〈보기〉 essential   materialistic   isolated

18 ＿＿＿＿＿＿＿＿＿ : attaching too much importance to money

19 ＿＿＿＿＿＿＿＿＿ : extremely important

20 ＿＿＿＿＿＿＿＿＿ : feeling lonely and without friends

Unit
03

요약문의
완성

✕ 유형 소개

1. 주어진 글을 읽고 글에 대한 요약문을 완성하는 유형이다.
2. 요약문은 대개 한 문장으로 이루어지며 핵심어에 해당하는 부분 두 군데가 빈칸으로 제시된다. 이 빈칸에 들어갈 적절한 말을 찾는 문제이다.
3. 어떤 글에 대한 요약문은 결국 주제나 요지에 해당하므로 주제나 요지 찾기 유형의 변형이라고 볼 수 있다.

✕ 유형 전략

Step 1 대의 파악을 위해 무엇에 관한 글인지, 글의 전체적인 의미가 무엇인지 반문하면서 읽는다.

Step 2 세부사항들은 빠르게 읽되, 주제나 요지와의 연관성에 주목한다.

Step 3 미완성의 요약문을 읽고, 본문에서 파악한 요지와 일치하도록 빈칸에 필요한 말을 고른다.

Words & Phrases

affordable (가격이) 알맞은
cough 기침
cultivate 재배하다
destructive 파괴적인
die out 멸종되다, 자취를 감추다
disease 질병
economy 경제
emperor 황제
empire 제국
enhance 드높이다, 증강하다
fatal 치명적인
globalize 세계화하다
growth 성장

impact 영향, 충격
income 소득, 수입
ingredient 재료
instead 대신
population 인구, 거주민
priority 우선
resident 거주민
solution 해결책
spread 확산; 확산시키다
strict 엄격한
treat 치료하다; 다루다
vast 막대한
weapon 무기

Example

다음 글의 내용을 한 문장으로 요약할 때 빈칸 (A)와 (B)에 들어갈 말로 가장 적절한 것은?

Garlic is an important ingredient in many cooking traditions. It has come to be widely used in all types of cooking, from Italian to Chinese. Used to season soups, stews, sauces, and dressing, garlic is now highly regarded throughout the world for its flavor and aroma. It is believed that Egyptians fed garlic to the slaves building the great pyramids to keep up their strength and stamina and prevent illnesses, such as colds, coughs, and viral infections. The plant has been cultivated for thousands of years in Asia and Europe and now grows in vast amounts in California.

> For thousands of years, garlic has been used for not only _____(A)_____ but also _____(B)_____ purposes.

	(A)	(B)		(A)	(B)
①	health	⋯⋯ exercising	②	health	⋯⋯ medicinal
③	spicy	⋯⋯ educational	④	culinary	⋯⋯ medicinal
⑤	culinary	⋯⋯ educational			

✕ 문제 해결하기

Step 1 글의 전체적인 의미 파악하기
마늘은 음식에 널리 사용될 뿐만 아니라 질병 치료에도 사용했다는 글의 내용이며 요즘 몸에 좋은 식품에 관한 지문이 가끔 등장하므로 참고 바람.

Step 2 세부사항과 주제의 연결 고리 파악하기
마늘은 수프나 스튜나 드레싱을 양념하는 데 쓰려고 하며 아울러 노예들에게 체력을 유지하기 위해 마늘을 먹였다는 내용이 나온다.

Step 3 파악한 글의 요지와 요약문 비교하기
마늘이 요리와 치료에 둘 다 효용이 있다는 내용이므로 요약문이 이런 의미를 나타내도록 필요한 말이 무엇인지 생각한다.

---

garlic 마늘 ingredient 재료 tradition 전통. 관습 season 맛을 내다. 간을 맞추다 highly 매우. 고도로 regard 주목해서 보다; 존중하다 slave 노예 keep up 유지하다 strength 힘 prevent 막다(= guard) illness 병. 아동기 질환 cough 기침 viral 바이러스성의 infection 감염 plant 식물 cultivate 재배하다 vast 막대한 culinary 요리의

Throughout history, the development of civilization has had an impact on people's health. *By settling and living close to each other, people created the perfect environment for the spread of disease. Trade and war also spread disease. <u>Diseases carried by armies were often more destructive than their weapons.</u> For example, in 1520, the Spaniards brought smallpox to the Aztecs by accident. The disease quickly spread among the population. The people had no resistance and no idea how to treat it. In many cases, everyone in a house died. The emperor, along with many of the leaders of the army, died of smallpox. It killed more than half the population and led to the end of the empire.

*smallpox 천연두

1 윗글의 내용을 다음과 같이 한 문장으로 요약하고자 한다. 빈칸 (A)와 (B)에 들어갈 말로 가장 적절한 것은?

> The growth of early civilizations created a good environment for _____(A)_____ disease among people, and the fall of the Aztecs shows that a(n) _____(B)_____ disease could have been very destructive to the local people.

	(A)		(B)		(A)		(B)
①	treating	······	dangerous, fatal	②	spreading	······	new, foreign
③	treating	······	new, foreign	④	spreading	······	old, familiar
⑤	spreading	······	old, fatal				

서술형

2 밑줄 친 부분을 우리말로 옮기시오.

_____

Grammar Points!　전치사 + 동명사

by -ing(~함으로써), on -ing(~하자마자), in -ing(~할 때), without -ing(~하지 않고) 등의 표현에 유의한다.
By settling and **living** close to each other, ~. 정착하고 서로 가까이 붙어살게 됨으로써 ~.

impact 영향, 충격 settle 정착하다 spread 확산; 확산시키다 disease 질병 trade 교역, 무역 destructive 파괴적인 weapon 무기 Spaniard 스페인 사람 by accident 우연히 population 인구, 거주민 treat 치료하다; 다루다 emperor 황제 empire 제국 growth 성장 fatal 치명적인

As a culture, we have been spending less of our personal income on food over the past few decades. We are trained to shop around for the lowest prices. However, food is probably the best investment we can make in our own health. Even though some people would like to buy higher-quality food, such as organic produce, it is often placed far down on the list of spending priorities due to its price. Some shoppers simply want the most affordable items. Nevertheless, in the modern globalized economy, *low prices sometimes mean that food is being grown in an overseas country. If domestic farmers were to give up farming, it would harm national food security.

1 윗글의 내용을 다음과 같이 한 문장으로 요약하고자 한다. 빈칸 (A)와 (B)에 들어갈 말로 가장 적절한 것은?

> Even though many people nowadays want to buy _____(A)_____ either for economic reasons or out of a simple habit, it can _____(B)_____ your health and our food security.

	(A)		(B)		(A)		(B)
①	organic food	⋯⋯	ruin	②	organic food	⋯⋯	improve
③	cheaper food	⋯⋯	improve	④	high-quality food	⋯⋯	ruin
⑤	cheaper food	⋯⋯	ruin				

서술형

2 필자가 주장하는 바를 25자 내외의 우리말로 쓰시오.

_____

Grammar Points! 현재진행 수동태

『be being p.p.』는 현재진행 수동태로서 '～되고 있다'의 의미이다.
Low prices sometimes mean that food **is being grown** in an overseas country.
낮은 가격은 때때로 해당 식료품이 해외에서 재배되고 있다는 점을 의미한다.

income 소득, 수입 decade 십 년 shop around for ～을 보러 다니다 investment 투자 such as ～과 같은 organic 유기(농)의 priority 우선 due to ～ 때문에 affordable (가격이) 알맞은 globalize 세계화하다 economy 경제 domestic 국내의, 가정의 (↔ international 해외의) give up 포기하다 food security 식품 안전

Beijing has a very serious smog problem. When the haze is really bad, residents are even unable to see across the street. *For this reason, almost no city resident leaves home without face masks. Although cutting emissions is the right thing to do, the Chinese government has so far not wanted to impose any strict rules. The leaders worry that it would impact the country's economic growth negatively. Instead, they are seeking a few long-term solutions. One of them is a giant electrostatic "vacuum cleaner." However, this method is effective at cutting small patches of clear sky just big enough to allow residents to see the sun.

* electrostatic 정전기의

1 윗글의 내용을 다음과 같이 한 문장으로 요약하고자 한다. 빈칸 (A)와 (B)에 들어갈 말로 가장 적절한 것은?

> Unless Chinese leaders are willing to _____(A)_____ the number of sources of pollution in China and overlook any negative economic consequences of doing so, they could find it difficult to _____(B)_____ Beijing's smog problem.

	(A)		(B)			(A)		(B)
①	increase	⋯⋯	avoid		②	decrease	⋯⋯	increase
③	reduce	⋯⋯	resolve		④	cut	⋯⋯	seek
⑤	reduce	⋯⋯	experience					

서술형

2 밑줄 친 them이 가리키는 것을 윗글에서 찾아 쓰시오.

_____

Grammar Points!　　이중 부정

no, without 등의 부정어가 함께 쓰이면 이중 부정이 되어 긍정의 의미가 된다.
For this reason, almost **no** city resident leaves home **without** face masks.
= For this reason, almost **every** city resident leaves home **with** face masks.
이런 이유 때문에 마스크를 하지 않고 집을 나서는 주민들은 거의 없다.

haze 안개, 아지랑이　　resident 거주민　　so far 지금까지　　impose 부과하다　　strict 엄격한　　instead 대신　　long-term 장기의　　solution 해결책
vacuum cleaner 진공청소기　　effective 효과적인　　patch 조각; 구역　　overlook (잘못된 것을) 못 본 체하다　　consequence 결과

*It is uncertain how the fourth industrial revolution will bring about changes in our lives, including how relationships are formed and how people communicate. But a(n) (A) optimistic / pessimistic view is easy to find. Some argue that the technology revolution will collapse the middle class and widen the polarization between the rich and the poor. Others even predict that machines will rule mankind. Stephen Hawking and Elon Musk have warned of possible disasters caused by uncontrolled AI. So, will people be happier? A Stanford University report titled "Artificial Intelligence and Life in 2030" pointed out that AI technology will (B) lower / hike the prices of products and services and will lead to people becoming more rich. But most experts agreed that people should be cautious of vague optimism. Song Kyung-jin, President of the Institute for Global Economics, has said, "[결국 어떤 기술을 받을지 안 받을지 결정하는 건 바로 인간이다] and technologies that fail to put humanity at their center will die out." Regrettably, the debates over the fourth industrial revolution have been focused only on technological changes. The discussions should instead be more focused on improving social safety nets that can (C) reserve / resolve social and cultural conflicts that may come from technological changes.

* polarization 양극화

1 윗글의 제목으로 가장 적절한 것은?

① Will Human Jobs Disappear?

② Defining an Industrial Revolution

③ Dealing With Conflicts Between Generations

④ Negative Aspects of the Fourth Industrial Revolution

⑤ What Are Key Technologies in the Fourth Industrial Revolution?

2 윗글의 내용을 다음과 같이 한 문장으로 요약하고자 한다. 빈칸 (A)와 (B)에 들어갈 말로 가장 적절한 것은?

> Some experts see _____(A)_____ coming in the fourth industrial revolution, so _____(B)_____ and building up social safety nets will be put on the top, not focusing only on technological changes.

	(A)	(B)		(A)	(B)
①	tragedy	...... competitions	②	tragedy	...... humans
③	renovations	...... competitions	④	renovations	...... humans
⑤	hope	...... robots			

3 (A), (B), (C)의 각 네모 안에서 문맥에 맞는 낱말로 가장 적절한 것은?

	(A)	(B)	(C)		(A)	(B)	(C)
①	optimistic	...... lower	...... reserve	②	optimistic	...... hike	...... reserve
③	pessimistic	...... lower	...... reserve	④	pessimistic	...... hike	...... resolve
⑤	pessimistic	...... lower	...... resolve				

서술형

4 주어진 단어를 이용하여 윗글의 [우리말]에 맞도록 바르게 배열하시오.

> accept / in the end / a technology / decide on / to / whether / who / it / is / humans

---

Grammar Points! 간접의문문의 어순

의문문이 문장의 일부분을 이루어 명사적 역할을 하는 경우 이를 간접의문문이라고 한다.
간접의문문의 어순은 『의문사 + 주어 + 동사』이다.

It is uncertain **how** the fourth industrial revolution will bring about changes in our lives.
　　　　　　　　(의문사)　　　　(주어)　　　　　　(동사)

4차 산업혁명이 우리의 삶에 어떤 변화를 가져다줄지 불확실하다.

---

industrial revolution 산업혁명　relationship 관계　optimistic 낙관적인(↔ pessimistic 회의적인) (*cf.* optimism 낙관주의)　the middle class 중류층
disaster 재난　expert 전문가　be cautious of ~을 조심하다　vague 막연한, 희미한　humanity 인류, 인간성　die out 멸종되다, 자취를 감추다

Word Check　✖ ✖ ✖

정답 및 해설 p.06

[1-10] 영어는 우리말로, 우리말은 영어로 나타내시오.

1　income : _____

2　impose : _____

3　priority : _____

4　destructive : _____

5　strict : _____

6　경제 : _____

7　기침 : _____

8　영향, 충격 : _____

9　투자 : _____

10　인구 : _____

[11-13] 괄호 안에서 알맞은 말을 고르시오.

11　She made a (fatal / vague) mistake.

12　We should reduce greenhouse gas (permission / emissions).

13　To (raise / enhance) your creativity, learn something new.

[14-16] 빈칸에 들어갈 말을 〈보기〉에서 골라 알맞은 형태로 쓰시오.

〈보기〉 spread　　vast　　ingredients　　accident

14　I met her by _____ on the street.

15　He uses only the freshest _____ in his cooking.

16　Someone has been _____ the rumor.

[17-18] 다음 짝지어진 단어의 관계가 같도록 빈칸에 알맞은 말을 쓰시오.

17　dozen : twelve = decade : _____

18　achieve : achievement = grow : _____

[19-21] 다음의 뜻에 해당하는 단어를 〈보기〉에서 골라 쓰시오.

〈보기〉 domestic　　vast　　emperor

19　_____ : a man who rules an empire

20　_____ : involving the home, family, or one's own country

21　_____ : very great in size, amount, or extent

Unit
04

글의 목적

✕ 유형 소개

1. 글이 어떤 목적으로 쓰였는지, 즉 필자가 글을 통해 말하고자 하는 바를 파악하는 유형이다.
2. 글의 목적이 몇몇 어구를 통해 직접적으로 드러나 있는 글도 있지만 글 전체 내용을 읽고 추론해야 하는 경우도 있다.
3. 편지글, 광고문, 안내문, 기사문 등 다양한 종류의 글에서 출제되고 있다.

✕ 유형 전략

Step 1 글의 첫 부분과 선택지를 읽고 누구를 대상으로 하여 누가 쓴 글인지 대략적인 내용을 유추해 본다.

Step 2 글의 어딘가에 목적을 나타내는 어구가 있는지 주의하며 읽는다. 목적이 드러나는 단어가 없는 경우 문장들 속에 내포된 의미를 생각하며 글을 읽는다. (항의 불만의 글: sorry, disappointed, regret, shameful 등 / 감사의 글: appreciate, thank 등 / 요청의 글: ask, call for, demand, require 등 / 통보의 글: inform, notice 등)

Step 3 글의 마지막 부분에 글을 쓴 목적이 분명히 드러나거나 강조되는 경우가 많으므로 후반부에 집중한다.

Words & Phrases

allow 허락하다, 허가하다
amazing 깜짝 놀라게 하는
annual 매년의, 연례의
artificial 인공적인
aspect 양상, 측면
base ~에 기초하다
celebrate 경축하다, 기리다
collapse 쓰러지다, 붕괴하다
devastate 완전히 파괴하다
distribute 분배하다, 나누어주다 (= give out)
duty 임무
exhaustion 극도의 피로; 고갈

list 목록으로 나와 있다, 명부에 올리다
local 지역의
postpone 연기하다
product 제품
register 등록하다
species 종(種: 생물 분류의 기초 단위)
stand on end 똑바로 서다
store 저장하다
support 지지(하다)
take off 벗다
take place 일어나다, 발생하다
valid 유효한

Example

다음 글의 목적으로 가장 적절한 것은?

정답 및 해설 p.07

Now you can open doors not just with your keys or ID cards but also with your smartphone, using an app called SmartKey. It's based on Near Field Communication, or NFC, a way to send data wirelessly over short distances. Many smartphones already have NFC chips built in. Here's how SmartKey works. After installing the app, you register with a central server. In a hotel, for instance, the front desk would run that aspect. They'd confirm your smartphone as property of a guest and send you an encoded key that is valid only for the length of your stay. Then simply wave your phone over your room's lock, and the key is stored on your phone.

① 열쇠 도난 시 대처법을 알려주려고
② 최첨단 도난 방지 자물쇠를 홍보하려고
③ 새로 나온 스마트폰 모델을 소개하려고
④ 호텔 방문객들에게 출입 카드 사용법을 알려주려고
⑤ 열쇠 대용 스마트폰 응용프로그램을 소개하려고

✕ 문제 해결하기

Step 1 글의 서두와 선택지 먼저 읽기
열쇠 대신 SmartKey라는 app을 이용하여 스마트폰으로 문을 열 수 있다는 내용의 첫 문장을 통해 글의 주제를 파악한 다음 선택지를 훑어 읽는다. 반복적으로 등장하는 열쇠, 스마트폰과 같은 단어를 통해 열쇠를 대신하는 스마트폰 앱을 소개하는 글임을 알 수 있다.

Step 2 목적을 나타내는 어구 찾기
글 중반부의 Here's how SmartKey works.라는 문장에서 이글의 목적이 무엇인지 명백히 드러난다.

Step 3 글의 후반부에 집중하기
글의 후반부는 스마트키의 구체적인 사용법을 호텔을 예로 들어 설명하고 있다. 이 글과는 달리 글의 후반부에 가서야 목적이 드러나는 경우도 많으므로 글의 후반부에 집중하여 읽을 필요가 있다.

app 앱(application: 응용 프로그램의 줄임말) base ~에 기초하다 distance 거리 built in 내장되어, 설치되어 install 설치하다 register 등록하다 for instance 예를 들면 aspect 양상, 측면 confirm 확인하다 property 소유물, 재산 encode 암호로 바꾸다, 부호화하다 valid 유효한 length 길이 store 저장하다

*Have you ever heard that bats, bees, fungi, gorillas, and plankton are the top five most important species residing on our planet? In fact, it has been said that the effects of losing all five of those listed species would cause the deaths of millions of human and animal life within five to ten years. Don't allow this to happen. Please help us to preserve Mother Nature and her most precious living organisms, both mammals and nonmammals alike. <u>Should we fail</u>, human and animal life will be devastated. Should you know of an ecological crime, poaching, or anyone harming the environment, please report it to us immediately.

1 윗글의 목적으로 가장 적절한 것은?

① 지역사회의 환경 보호 운동을 치하하려고

② 학생들이 환경보호 캠페인에 동참하도록 권하려고

③ 환경에 해를 끼치는 행위에 대한 신고를 독려하려고

④ 멸종 위기에 처한 동식물에 대한 정보를 제공하려고

⑤ 생태계 보호를 위해 지켜야 할 행동 지침을 알리려고

서술형

2 밑줄 친 Should we fail에서 생략된 말을 살려 다시 쓰시오.

_____

Grammar Points!　　분사의 위치와 의미

명사를 수식하는 분사에 다른 어구가 붙어 있으면 분사는 그 명사 뒤에 온다. 이때 수식하는 명사와 능동 관계이면 현재분사가, 수동 관계이면 과거분사가 온다.

Have you ever heard that bats, bees, fungi, gorillas, and plankton are the top five most important **species residing on our planet**?

박쥐, 벌, 균류, 고릴라, 그리고 플랑크톤이 우리 행성에 살고 있는 가장 중요한 다섯 가지 종(種)이라는 말을 들어본 적이 있습니까?

fungi 균류(fungus의 복수 명사)　**species** 종(種: 생물 분류의 기초 단위)　**reside** 살다, 존재하다　**list** 목록으로 나와 있다, 명부에 올리다　**allow** 허락하다, 허가하다　**preserve** 보존하다, 보호하다 (n. preservation 보존)　**devastate** 완전히 파괴하다　**ecological** 생태계의　**crime** 범죄　**poach** 밀렵하다　**immediately** 즉시, 곧

You take off your cozy wool hat after being out in the winter cold, and your hair is standing on end. *Even if you put some water on it to calm it down for a moment, the static electricity always comes back. There are two main reasons for static in your hair. The first one is the winter season itself. The dry air, artificial heat and wool hats that come with winter make your hair and scalp dry out. The second reason is an overdose of products in your hair. So how can you keep your hair static-free this winter? Silky Diamond, our amazing hair lotion, has the key to keep your hair tamed!

1 윗글의 목적으로 가장 적절한 것은?

① 정전기가 생기는 원리를 설명하려고

② 정전기 방지 세탁법을 알려주려고

③ 건강한 모발 관리법을 소개해 주려고

④ 머릿결에 나쁜 습관들을 경고하려고

⑤ 정전기 방지 모발 제품을 홍보하려고

> 서술형

2 밑줄 친 Even if you put some water on it을 우리말로 옮기시오.

_____

Grammar Points! 양보의 뜻을 나타내는 접속사 even if

even if는 '~하더라도, ~일지라도'란 뜻의 양보를 나타내는 접속사이며, 같은 뜻으로 although, though가 있다.

Even if you put some water on it to calm it down for a moment, the static electricity always comes back. 당신이 그것을 잠시 진정시키기 위해 물을 좀 뿌린다 하더라도 정전기는 항상 다시 생깁니다.

---

take off 벗다 cozy 아늑한, 포근한 stand on end 똑바로 서다 for a moment 잠시 static electricity 정전기 artificial 인공적인 scalp 두피
overdose 과다복용(투여) (over(~보다 많은)+dose(복용량)) product 제품 static-free 정전기가 없는 amazing 깜짝 놀라게 하는 tame 길들이다

The promotions review meeting originally ⓐ (schedule) for the first week of May has been postponed for one month due to the sudden illness of Mr. William Blake. As I am sure that you are all aware, Mr. Blake collapsed during the annual company festival last week. He was taken to Mercy Hospital and the doctors have said that the reason for his collapse was simple exhaustion. The prognosis is good and he is expected to fully recover in about three weeks. He will be able to start his duties again in about a month. Everyone is encouraged to send flowers and get-well cards either individually or as a department, but *visitations are currently being limited to immediate family members.

* prognosis 의사의 소견, 예후

1 다음 글을 쓴 목적으로 가장 적절한 것은?

① 회사 창립일 행사를 안내하려고
② 올해 승진 시험 일자를 공고하려고
③ 병문안 할 때의 유의사항을 알리려고
④ 승진심사위원회의 심의 결과를 알리려고
⑤ 입원한 동료에게 꽃 보낼 것을 권유하려고

서술형

2 ⓐ (schedule)를 어법에 맞게 알맞게 고쳐 쓰시오.

_____

Grammar Points!　진행형 수동태

진행형 수동태는 진행형인 문장의 수동태형을 말하며, 그 형태는 『be ~ing → be being p.p.』이다.
Visitations **are** currently **being limited** to immediate family members. (수동형)
→ They **are** currently **limiting** visitations to immediate family members. (능동형)
현재로서는 직계가족 이외에는 방문이 허용되지 않습니다.

promotion review meeting 승진심사위원회　be scheduled for ~로 예정되다　postpone 연기하다　collapse 쓰러지다. 붕괴하다　annual 매년의, 연례의　be taken to ~로 후송되다　exhaustion 극도의 피로; 고갈　duty 일. 임무　get-well card 쾌유카드　currently 현재　limit A to B A를 B로 제한하다　immediate family member 직계가족

Bullying is one of the most serious social problems that can lead victims to death. It can take place anywhere — at school, at home, and online — and it's important to speak up about it. You can stand against bullying without saying a word. Simply slip into a pink T-shirt on Pink Shirt Day, February 26.

(A)

Two high school students in Nova Scotia, Canada, started Pink Shirt Day after witnessing a new classmate getting bullied for wearing a pink shirt to school. A light bulb went off for David Shepherd and Travis Price, and they ran to their local dollar store. They bought up all the pink shirts they could find and distributed them to everyone at their school, showing the bullies that bullying wasn't okay.

(B)

Students, schools, offices, and whoever wants to join can now celebrate Pink Shirt Day as a way to speak up about bullying. *It takes place every February, and all you need to do to take part is put on some pink! There are lots of different ways to show your support for Pink Shirt Day and to get your friends and school involved, too. Bullying is a serious issue, and Pink Shirt Day can be a great way to get a discussion started with everyone you know.

1 윗글의 목적으로 가장 적절한 것은?

① 집단괴롭힘 피해자의 사례를 수집하려고

② 집단괴롭힘 추방 캠페인 동참을 촉구하려고

③ 집단괴롭힘 현상의 심리학적 연구 결과를 알리려고

④ 성공한 사회 운동의 영향력을 설명하려고

⑤ 학생들이 참여하면 좋을 교내 활동을 홍보하려고

2 윗글의 빈칸 (A)와 (B)에 들어갈 알맞은 제목을 〈보기〉에서 골라 기호를 쓰시오.

> 〈보기〉 a. How Do I Get Involved?
> b. How Did Pink Shirt Day Originate?
> c. Why Do You Have to Wear a Pink Shirt?
> d. What Has the Pink Shirt Day Brought About?

(A) _____   (B) _____

3 다음 중 Pink Shirt Day에 관한 내용으로 <u>틀린</u> 것은?

① Two high school students started it to stand up against bullying.

② Anyone can take part in the campaign by wearing a pink shirt.

③ Bullies are supposed to wear a pink shirt to show their regrets.

④ Pink Shirt Day takes place on February 26 every year.

⑤ It can serve as a warning to stop bullying in our society.

서술형

4 밑줄 친 <u>whoever wants to join</u>을 다음 주어진 단어로 시작하여 바꾸어 쓰시오.

= anyone _____

Grammar Points! **목적격 관계대명사의 생략**

관계대명사가 이끄는 절에서 관계대명사가 목적어일 경우 이를 목적격 관계대명사라고 하는데, 이 목적격 관계대명사는 생략할 수 있다.

It takes place every February, and all **(that)** you need to do to take part is put on some pink!

그것은 매년 2월에 있으며, 참가하기 위해 당신이 해야 하는 일이라곤 분홍색을 입는 것뿐이다!

---

bullying 집단괴롭힘(cf. bully (약한 자를) 들볶다; 불량배)   victim 피해자   take place 일어나다, 발생하다   slip into (옷을) 걸쳐 입다   a light bulb goes off 좋은 아이디어가 생각나다   local 지역의   distribute 분배하다, 나누어주다 (= give out)   celebrate 경축하다, 기리다   take part 참석하다, 참여하다 (= participate)   support 지지(하다)   involve 참여시키다, 포함하다

Word Check ✖ ✖ ✖

[1-10] **영어는 우리말로, 우리말은 영어로 나타내시오.**

1　register : _____

2　confirm : _____

3　valid : _____

4　store : _____

5　reside : _____

6　피해자 : _____

7　경축하다, 기리다 : _____

8　설치하다 : _____

9　유기체, 생물 : _____

10　생태계의 : _____

[11-13] **괄호 안에서 알맞은 말을 고르시오.**

11　Don't waste (precious / worthless) time playing the computer games.

12　This ticket is (based / valid) on the day of issue only.

13　I'm calling you to (commit / confirm) my order.

[14-16] **빈칸에 들어갈 말을 〈보기〉에서 골라 알맞은 형태로 쓰시오.**

〈보기〉 register　　devastate　　confirm

14　The flood _____ the town.

15　She _____ her new car.

16　Rumours were later _____.

[17-18] **다음 짝지어진 단어의 관계가 같도록 빈칸에 알맞은 말을 쓰시오.**

17　wide : width = long : _____

18　natural : artificial = destroy : _____

[19-21] **다음의 뜻에 해당하는 단어를 〈보기〉에서 골라 쓰시오.**

〈보기〉 distribute　　collapse　　artificial

19　_____ : hand or deliver something to a number of people

20　_____ : not natural or real

21　_____ : to break apart and fall down suddenly

Unit 05

빈칸 추론

✕ 유형 소개

1. 주어진 글을 읽고 빈칸에 들어갈 말을 유추하는 문제 유형이다.
2. 글을 정확하게 읽고, 제시된 문맥을 바탕으로 글의 논리를 파악할 수 있는지를 확인하는 평가이다.
3. 가장 출제 비중이 높지만 학생들이 가장 어려워하는 유형이기도 하다.

✕ 유형 전략

Step 1 빈칸이 있는 문장이 글의 주제나 요지, 주장에 해당할 경우 글의 세부 내용들을 빠르게 읽고 주제나 요지 등을 파악한다.

Step 2 빈칸이 있는 문장이 세부사항이라면 글을 끝까지 읽고 주제를 파악한 후, 빈칸이 있는 문장의 세부 내용과 어떻게 연관되는지 파악한다.

Step 3 빈칸 문제는 논리적인 유추가 필요한 만큼 therefore, however, in addition 같은 논리적 연결사에도 주목한다.

Words & Phrases

appeal 호소하다
area 분야; 지역
as a result 결과적으로
atmosphere 대기; 분위기
career 직업; 경력
comfortable 편안한
digest 소화하다 (*n.* digestion 소화)
entertain 즐겁게 하다
especially 특히
global warming 지구 온난화
hold 신봉하다, 주장하다
impression 인상
in addition 게다가

item 품목, 항목
medicine 의학; 약
precious 소중한, 귀중한
profession (지적) 직업
provide 제공하다
religion 종교
replace 되돌리다; 대체하다
set up 세우다
stability 안전성, 부동성
thrive 번창하다
trap 덫으로 잡다
treat 대하다, 취급하다

Example

Historically, the growth of the university system shows _____. For around five hundred years, schools had remained in the hands of the churches. These schools were only interested in teaching religion. However, the middle class needed to know mathematics, medicine, and natural sciences for their trades. Furthermore, the sons of the wealthy middle class hoped to rise in the Church, in government, and in professions. Schools were needed to prepare these young men for a new future.

For this reason, the middle class set up associations, or "universities," of students and masters.

① the fall of religion
② the development of democratic ideas
③ the establishment of the middle class
④ the beginning of the dispute between religion and science
⑤ people's recognition of the importance of education

✕ 문제 해결하기

Step 1 **세부 내용을 통해 주제나 요지를 파악하기**
빈칸 문장이 글의 맨 앞에 온 데다가 전반적이고 포괄적인 언급으로 시작하고 있으므로 주제문임을 예측할 수 있다. 이어지는 세부 내용들은 middle class가 어떤 필요에 의해서 "universities"를 세우게 됐는지에 관한 설명들이다.

Step 2 **연결사에 주목하기**
However를 통해 교회와 대비되는 세력의 등장을, Furthermore를 통해 중산층이 새로운 학교를 원하는 이유가 계속 열거될 것임을, For this reason을 통해 결말이 나올 것임을 예측할 수 있다.

Step 3 **답안 확인하기**
윗글은 역사적으로 대학교가 생겨나게 된 배경을 설명하는 글로서 중산층의 등장이 가져온 대학의 발전이 주제에 해당한다.

---

religion 종교 medicine 의학; 약 trade 거래하다 furthermore 게다가 profession (지적) 직업 prepare 준비하다 set up 세우다 master 스승 democratic 민주주의적인 establishment 설립, 확립 dispute 논쟁, 분쟁

*Though entertaining, soap operas can give the wrong impression about _____. In soap operas the characters are usually attractive and rich. For example, in popular soap operas, people live in big houses with expensive furniture, sometimes on the beach. Even the characters who are supposed to be in college are rich. In contrast, most people in our country are middle class. Their jobs are often dull, their houses are comfortable but not fancy, and their cars are usually several years old. In addition, most college students have to work to support themselves.

1 윗글의 빈칸에 가장 알맞은 말은?

① human relationships

② how people in our country live

③ how people connect art and life

④ how college students earn money

⑤ rich people's attitudes toward poor people

서술형

2 윗글은 soap operas의 어떤 점을 비판하고 있는지 5자 이내의 우리말로 쓰시오.

_____

Grammar Points! 　부사절에서 『주어 + be동사』의 생략

부사절에서 주어가 주절의 주어와 같고, 동사가 be동사일 경우 부사절에서 『주어 + be동사』를 생략할 수 있다.

Though (**they are**) entertaining, <u>soap operas</u> can give the wrong impression about ~.

비록 재미는 있지만 멜로드라마는 ~에 대한 잘못된 인상을 줄 수 있다.

entertain 즐겁게 하다　soap opera 멜로드라마　impression 인상　attractive 매력적인 (v. attract 끌다, 매혹하다)　be supposed to ~하기로 되어 있다　in contrast 대조적으로, 반대로　dull 지루한　comfortable 편안한　fancy 화려한, 값비싼　in addition 게다가　relationship 관계

PRACTICE 2

Like other greenhouse gases, methane helps to keep the Earth's heat trapped in our atmosphere, and the temperature of the Earth goes up as a result. Humans are not the only producers of methane; cows also produce it while digesting their food. However, as we learn more about the causes of the greenhouse effect, *we now know cows are far less guilty of contributing to global warming than humans and cars are. The amount of methane produced by cows adds up to about 3 percent of the total amount of greenhouse gases produced by people. _____ _____ won't solve the world's warming problem.

* methane 메탄

1 윗글의 빈칸에 가장 적절한 것은?

① Reducing methane
② Getting a cow to change its diet
③ Cooling the atmosphere of the earth
④ Scientific research in the laboratory
⑤ Human efforts, however sincere they are,

서술형

2 주어진 말을 알맞은 형태로 바꾸어 빈칸에 써넣으시오.

We should keep the child _____ 24 hours a day. (protect)

Grammar Points! 비교급을 강조하는 말

'훨씬, 더욱' 등의 의미로 비교급을 강조할 때 far, even, much 등을 써서 나타낸다.
We now know cows are **far** less guilty of contributing to global warming than humans and cars are. 이제 우리는 소가 지구온난화에 이바지하는 죄는 인간과 자동차보다 훨씬 덜하다는 걸 안다.

---

greenhouse gas 온실가스   trap 덫으로 잡다   atmosphere 대기; 분위기   as a result 결과적으로   digest 소화하다 (*n.* digestion 소화)   cause 원인
greenhouse effect 온실 효과   be guilty of ~의 죄를 범하다   contribute to ~에 이바지하다   global warming 지구온난화   add up to 합계 ~가
되다   solve 해결하다   reduce 줄이다   laboratory 실험실

What does the new business environment mean for you, your education, and your career choices? A fast-changing business environment creates fast-growing careers while at the same time it turns other careers into dead ends. The <u>conventional wisdom</u> holds that the wisest course is to pick a field that is on the upswing. The conventional wisdom is right to a degree. However, in a fast-changing environment you cannot count on stability. Today's hot careers may soon be dead ends replaced by tomorrow's hot careers. Therefore, if you want to succeed, *you must first consider what you want to do and what you are good at, and then develop a set of all-purpose job skills that _____.

1 윗글의 빈칸에 가장 적절한 것은?

① can make you the best at your job

② traditional businessmen had in the past

③ you can transfer to the next growth area

④ you will need to educate future businessmen

⑤ will let you know at which skill you are strong

서술형

2 밑줄 친 conventional wisdom이 가리키는 내용을 우리말로 쓰시오.

_____

Grammar Points!　　**what이 이끄는 의문사절**

의문사 what이 이끄는 절이 문장의 목적어가 될 경우 '무엇이/무엇을 ~하는지를'이라고 해석한다.
You must consider first what you want to do and what you are good at.
당신은 먼저 당신이 원하는 것은 무엇이고 무엇을 잘 하는지를 고려해야 한다.

---

environment 환경　**career** 직업; 경력　**dead end** 막다름, 막힌 끝　**conventional** 관습적인, 재래의　**hold** 신봉하다, 주장하다　**upswing** 상승, 발전　**to a degree** 다소간, 약간　**count on** ~을 의지하다, 기대하다　**stability** 안정성, 부동성 (*a.* stable 안정된, 견고한)　**replace** 되돌리다; 대체하다　**a set of** 일련의　**all-purpose** 다목적의, 만능의　**transfer** 옮기다, 이동하다　**area** 분야; 지역

Many new markets have appeared to meet the needs of *pet owners ① <u>who</u> treat their pets as if they were precious children. The market thriving most is pet clothing, especially items that allow owners and their dogs to ② <u>dress</u> alike. Designer clothing for pets and their owners is the fastest-growing segment of this market. Another big market ③ <u>is made up of</u> hotels all over the world that advertise themselves as pet friendly. These hotels provide guests with dog and cat beds, on-site grooming, and pet-care professionals. Many of these hotels don't even allow children, but they welcome pets. I recently saw an ad for a hotel ④ <u>which</u> has rooms that the owners can choose for their dogs to stay in while they are away. The rooms are uniquely ⑤ <u>decorating</u>, and the packages include special meals prepared and served to meet the needs of each "guest." These new markets don't cater to <u>the conservative spender</u>; they appeal to those pet owners who seem willing to _____.

1 윗글의 제목으로 가장 적절한 것은?

① Why Do People Keep Pets?
② Special Hotels for Cats and Dogs
③ Businesses Booming as Pets Join the Family
④ Pets Are the Best Friends of Lonely People
⑤ Designer Fashion Markets Always Prosper

2 윗글의 빈칸에 들어갈 말로 가장 적절한 것은?

① care for their pets themselves
② travel with their pets wherever they go
③ spend any amount of money for their pets
④ dress their pets up like humans
⑤ spend time with their pets whenever possible

3 윗글의 밑줄 친 ①~⑤ 중, 어법상 틀린 것은?

①   ②   ③   ④   ⑤

서술형

4 윗글로 보아 밑줄 친 <u>the conservative spender</u>는 누구를 가리키는지 20자 내외의 우리말로 답하시오.

_____

Grammar Points!　　**as if 가정법**

'마치 ~인 것처럼'의 의미인 as if는 가정법 시제로 나타낸다. 즉, 현재의 사실을 반대로 가정할 땐 『as if + S + were/과거 동사』로, 과거의 사실을 반대하여 가정할 땐 『as if + S + had p.p.』로 표현한다.
Pet owners treat their pets as if they were precious children.
애완동물의 주인들은 그들의 애완동물을 마치 소중한 자식인 것처럼 대한다.

appear ~인 것 같다　meet 충족시키다　treat 대하다, 취급하다　precious 소중한, 귀중한　thrive 번창하다　especially 특히　item 품목, 항목
designer 유명 브랜드의, 유명 디자이너가 만든　segment 부분, 구획　be made up of ~으로 구성되다　provide 제공하다　on-site 현장의　groom
(동물을) 손질하다, 다듬다　ad (= advertisement) 광고　uniquely 독특하게 (a. unique 독특한)　cater to ~에 응하다　conservative 보수적인　appeal
호소하다

Word Check ✕ ✕ ✕

정답 및 해설 p.09

[1-10] 영어는 우리말로, 우리말은 영어로 나타내시오.

1 profession : _____

2 advertise : _____

3 trap : _____

4 conservative : _____

5 replace : _____

6 직업; 경력 : _____

7 번창하다 : _____

8 화려한, 값비싼 : _____

9 인상 : _____

10 소화하다 : _____

[11-13] 괄호 안에서 알맞은 말을 고르시오.

11 He divided the orange into (selections / segments).

12 There was a(n) (atmosphere / temperature) of distrust among the members.

13 He (holds / meets) that the theory is incorrect.

[14-17] 빈칸에 들어갈 말을 〈보기〉에서 골라 알맞은 형태로 쓰시오.

> 〈보기〉 meet   count   unique   add

14 You can _____ on my help.

15 They don't have money to _____ expenses.

16 He speaks English with a _____ accent.

17 For a hit show, profits can _____ up to millions.

18 **밑줄 친 부분과 바꿔 쓸 수 있는 말을 고르시오.**

> Those are <u>precious</u> objects that belong to her mother.

① interesting   ② valuable   ③ strange   ④ antique

[19-21] 다음의 뜻에 해당하는 단어를 〈보기〉에서 골라 쓰시오.

> 〈보기〉 conventional   support   appeal

19 _____ : to hold in position so as to keep from falling, to give aid

20 _____ : to ask for; to be attractive or interesting

21 _____ : following the accepted customs or standards

Unit
06
___
연결사 추론

※ 유형 소개

1. 단락 내 각 문장은 서로 논리적으로 연관되어 있는데 연결사는 이러한 문장들을 논리적으로 연결시켜 주는 말이다.
2. 빈칸에 들어갈 연결사를 추론하는 문제는 글을 읽고 논리적 사고의 흐름을 파악할 수 있는지 평가하기 위한 유형이다.
3. 주제문을 바탕으로 단락의 전개 방식을 예측하고 문장 간의 논리적 관계를 정확히 파악해야 해결할 수 있는 문제로서 한 지문 안에 두 개의 연결사를 추론하는 유형으로 출제되고 있다.

※ 유형 전략

Step 1 글의 도입부를 읽고 무엇에 관해 말하고자 하는 글인지, 글이 어떤 방식으로 전개될지 파악한다.

Step 2 빈칸 앞뒤에 위치한 문장 간의 논리적 관계를 파악한 후 적절한 연결사를 고른다.

Step 3 선택한 연결사를 빈칸에 대입하여 의미가 자연스럽게 연결되는지 확인한다.

Words & Phrases

accident 사고, 사건
argue 논쟁하다, 주장하다
attitude 태도, 자세
current 현재의
demand 요구하다
equal 대등한 사람; 동일한
fantasy 환상, 공상
freedom 자유
immediately 즉시
increase 증가시키다, 증가하다
infection 감염
lack 부재, 결핍
link 연결하다

necessarily 필연적으로, 반드시
occasion 경우, 때
oxygen 산소
particular 특정의
pressure 압력
properly 적절하게
root 뿌리, 근거
science fiction 공상과학 소설
subject 주제
suppose 가정하다
suspect 의심하다
traditional 전통의
warn 경고하다

Example

다음 글의 빈칸 (A), (B)에 들어갈 말로 가장 적절한 것은?

정답 및 해설 p.10

When you are stressed, the powerful hormones adrenaline and cortisol move quickly through your body. The hormones increase your heart rate, blood pressure, blood sugar, and need for oxygen. These are the changes that help people get through stressful situations successfully. _____(A)_____, when stress is out of your control, your body's immune system suffers. This is a problem for many people. _____(B)_____, 75% to 90% of all visits to the doctor's office are stress-related.

* adrenaline 아드레날린   * cortisol 코르티솔 (부신 피질 호르몬의 일종)

	(A)		(B)
①	However	–	In fact
②	Therefore	–	For example
③	In addition	–	As a result
④	First of all	–	In short
⑤	On the other hand	–	Instead

✕ 문제 해결하기

Step 1 **도입부를 통해 글의 주제 파악**
첫 두 문장을 통해 이 글은 스트레스를 받을 때 분비되는 호르몬에 관한 내용임을 알 수 있다.

Step 2 **빈칸 앞뒤 문장 간의 논리적 관계 파악하기**
빈칸 (A)의 앞 문장 내용은 '스트레스를 극복하기 위한 인체의 변화'이고 뒤 문장 내용은 '통제 불능의 스트레스가 인체에 미치는 악영향'이므로 둘의 논리적 관계는 〈대조〉임을 알 수 있다. 빈칸 (B)의 앞 문장 내용은 '스트레스로 인한 면역 이상 문제를 겪는 사람들'이고 뒤 문장은 '환자 대다수가 스트레스 때문'이라는 내용이므로 뒤 문장은 앞 문장의 〈부연 설명〉임을 알 수 있다. 이러한 논리적 관계를 바탕으로 알맞은 연결사끼리 짝지어진 선택지를 고른다.

Step 3 **선택한 연결사를 빈칸에 대입해보기**
선택한 선택지의 연결사를 각각 넣어 보고 글의 흐름이 자연스러운지 확인해 본다.

increase 증가시키다, 증가하다   heart rate 심박동 수   pressure 압력   blood sugar 혈당   oxygen 산소   get through 극복하다, ~을 끝내다   out of control 제어할 수 없는   immune 면역의   suffer 고통받다, ~을 앓다   related 관련된 (v. relate 관계시키다)

Each year lots of people die of infections they caught while in the hospital. The number of these kinds of hospital deaths is much more than that of the deaths on US highways. The cause of the deaths is unsanitary conditions in the hospitals. * The floors and doors in the hospitals might not be cleaned thoroughly. *Cooks and food handlers can easily infect food by not washing properly. Doctors might put on gloves without washing their hands first. _____(A)_____, the germs on their hands are transferred to the outside of the gloves. _____(B)_____, consumer groups warn patients to demand cleanliness. If patients see or suspect poor hygiene, they must tell someone immediately. It could be a matter of life or death.

1 윗글의 빈칸 (A), (B)에 들어갈 말로 가장 적절한 것은?

(A)		(B)
① In other words	–	However
② For example	–	Therefore
③ As a result	–	Thus
④ In contrast	–	Accordingly
⑤ In addition	–	Moreover

서술형
2 밑줄 친 that이 가리키는 명사를 찾아 쓰시오.

_____

Grammar Points! 부정어 not의 위치

조동사가 있는 수동태에서 부정어 not의 위치는 조동사 다음이며, 동명사에 대한 부정은 동명사 바로 앞에 위치한다.

The floors and doors in the hospitals <u>might</u> **not** be cleaned thoroughly. (조동사 다음)
병원의 바닥과 문들은 철저하게 청소되지 않을 것이다.

Cooks and food handlers can easily infect food by **not** <u>washing</u> properly. (동명사 앞)
요리사와 음식 취급자들은 적절하게 씻지 않아서 음식을 쉽게 감염시킬 수 있다.

---

die of ~로 인해 죽다   **infection** 감염   **unsanitary** 비위생적인, 불결한 (↔ sanitary 위생적인)   **handler** 손으로 만지는 사람 (v. handle 다루다, 조작하다)   **infect** 감염시키다   **properly** 적절하게   **germ** 세균   **consumer** 소비자 (v. consume 소비하다)   **warn** 경고하다   **demand** 요구하다   **cleanliness** 청결(함)   **suspect** 의심하다   **hygiene** 위생학, 위생상태   **immediately** 즉시

Would you want to travel to the future to see all the changes that will occur? Would you come back to the present and warn people of future earthquakes or accidents? Remember that if you came back 1000 years later, all the people you knew would be gone. *These ideas, first presented in a novel called *The Time Machine*, written by H.G. Wells over one hundred years ago, are the subject not only of fantasy but of serious scientific exploration. _____(A)_____, many of today's scientific discoveries and explorations had their roots in science fiction novels and movies. _____(B)_____ most physicists believe that travel to the future is possible, many believe that travel to the past will never happen.

1 윗글의 빈칸 (A), (B)에 들어갈 말로 가장 적절한 것은?

(A)		(B)
① However	–	Though
② For instance	–	Because
③ In contrast	–	Since
④ In fact	–	While
⑤ Furthermore	–	As

서술형
2 밑줄 친 부분을 우리말로 옮기시오.

_____

Grammar Points!　　상관접속사 not only A but (also) B

'A뿐만 아니라 B도'라는 의미의 상관접속사이다. 같은 의미로 〈B as well as A〉를 쓸 수 있다.
These ideas are the subject **not only** of fantasy **but** of serious scientific exploration.
이러한 생각들은 공상의 주제일 뿐만 아니라 진지한 과학 탐구의 주제이기도 하다.

---

occur 일어나다, 발생하다 (= take place)　present 현재; 나타나다　earthquake 지진　accident 사고, 사건　subject 주제　fantasy 환상, 공상
serious 진지한　exploration 탐험, 조사 (v. explore 탐험하다, 탐구하다)　root 뿌리, 근거　physicist 물리학자

*As personal freedom has increased in the modern world, social and moral attitudes have become less strict. This has allowed for a greater variety of lifestyles and freedom in human relations. Pupils and teachers now treat each other as equals, and parent-child relationships are now much more relaxed. _____(A)_____, some people believe that this increase in freedom has resulted in the escalation of social problems. They argue that the current lack of discipline has given rise to a breakdown in the traditional family and the decay in educational standards as well as the rise in teenage misbehavior. _____(B)_____, it may be said that <u>society is becoming more and more dangerous</u> because of the very fact that people are more open-minded than they were in the past.

1 윗글의 빈칸 (A), (B)에 들어갈 말로 가장 적절한 것은?

	(A)		(B)
①	Instead	–	On the other hand
②	As a result	–	In contrast
③	However	–	Otherwise
④	Likewise	–	Consequently
⑤	Nevertheless	–	Therefore

서술형

2 밑줄 친 부분을 society(주어)로 시작하도록 바꿔 쓰시오.

society _____

Grammar Points! **부사절의 접속사 as**

부사절의 접속사로 쓰이는 as의 주요 의미에는 '~할 때, ~함에 따라서, ~이므로, ~하는 대로' 등이 있다.

As personal freedom has increased in the modern world, social and moral attitudes have become less strict. 현대 세계에서 개인의 자유가 증가함에 따라 사회적, 도덕적 태도는 덜 엄격해졌다.

---

freedom 자유 **moral** 도덕의 (↔ immoral 부도덕한) **attitude** 태도, 자세 **strict** 엄한, 엄격한 **variety** 다양성 (a. various 다양한) **treat** 대하다, 대우하다 **equal** 대등한 사람; 동일한 **result in** ~을 야기하다 (cf. result from ~로부터 야기되다) **escalation** 점진적 증가, 단계적 확대 **argue** 논쟁하다, 주장하다 **current** 현재의 **lack** 부재, 결핍 **give rise to** ~을 야기하다 **breakdown** 몰락, 붕괴 **traditional** 전통의 **misbehavior** 나쁜 행실

*The information that is emphasized on one occasion is not necessarily stressed on another occasion. Context determines how you experience and encode information. Accordingly, context is a major factor in determining how closely linked your memory code for an experience is to a particular retrieval cue.   (A)   , suppose you went to a concert, and the most important parts of the experience to you were that your friend made you wait so long that you missed the first half-hour and that you ended up standing by the door because the seats were so bad. Two years later, when your friend says, "Do you remember that time we were at a concert and we ran into that woman from Telecom during the interval?", you are not likely to remember this event from this recall cue. Assuming you had been to a number of concerts together, this is not likely to be a great cue.   (B)   , if your friend says, "Remember that concert we were so late for? — You were so grumpy," that is much more likely to do the trick.

* retrieval cue (심리학) 인출 단서(머릿속에 저장된 정보를 불러오도록 도와주는 매개체)

1 윗글의 빈칸 (A), (B)에 들어갈 말로 가장 적절한 것은?

	(A)		(B)
①	In the same way	–	Hence
②	For example	–	On the other hand
③	Therefore	–	However
④	Instead	–	Consequently
⑤	For instance	–	Moreover

2 다음 중 윗글의 요지로 가장 적절한 것은?

① 기억은 그때의 정황에 따라 왜곡되어 저장된다.

② 사건의 정황이 기억을 저장하는 방식에 영향을 준다.

③ 같은 사건이라도 대응 방식은 사람마다 다르다.

④ 불쾌한 경험이 가장 오랫동안 기억 속에 저장된다.

⑤ 사람마다 정보를 저장하는 고유의 방식을 갖고 있다.

서술형

3 윗글에서 언급된 두 가지 retrieval cue의 구체적인 예를 우리말로 쓰시오.

_____

서술형

4 밑줄 친 문장을 다음과 같이 전환할 때 빈칸에 알맞은 말을 쓰시오.

Remember that concert for _____?

Grammar Points!　**부분 부정**

부정어 not이 전체나 필수를 의미하는 all, every, both, always, necessarily 등의 말에 연이어 쓰이면 '모두/둘 다/항상/반드시 ~한 것은 아니다'라는 부분 부정의 의미가 된다.

The information that is emphasized on one occasion is **not necessarily** stressed on another occasion. 하나의 경우에 강조된 정보가 다른 경우에도 반드시 강조되지는 않는다.

emphasize 강조하다　occasion 경우, 때　necessarily 필연적으로, 반드시　stress 강조하다　determine 결정하다 (= decide)　particular 특정의 suppose 가정하다　end up -ing 결국 ~로 끝나다　run into 우연히 마주치다, (곤경 등을) 만나다, 겪다　interval (극장 등의) 막간, 휴게 시간　recall 회상, 상기　assume 당연한 것으로 여기다, 추정하다　grumpy 기분이 언짢은　do the trick 성공하다, 효험이 있다

Word Check ✖ ✖ ✖

정답 및 해설 p.11

[1-10] 영어는 우리말로, 우리말은 영어로 나타내시오.

1   escalation : _____

2   hygiene : _____

3   attitude : _____

4   decay : _____

5   grumpy : _____

6   세균 : _____

7   막간, 휴게 시간 : _____

8   전후 사정, 상황 : _____

9   경우, 때 : _____

10   물리학자 : _____

[11-13] 괄호 안에서 알맞은 말을 고르시오.

11   He failed to reach the required (subject / standard), and did not qualify for the race.

12   The (current / moral) fad among teenagers is to wear skinny pants.

13   It is unreasonable to (assume / recall) that the economy will continue to improve.

[14-16] 빈칸에 들어갈 말을 〈보기〉에서 골라 알맞은 형태로 쓰시오.

〈보기〉 get through   give rise to   run into

14   This event may _____ serious trouble.

15   You just have to _____ these difficult times.

16   We probably _____ him every day on the street.

[17-18] 다음 짝지어진 단어의 관계가 같도록 빈칸에 알맞은 말을 쓰시오.

17   happen : occur = decide : _____

18   infect : infection = explore : _____

[19-21] 다음의 뜻에 해당하는 단어를 〈보기〉에서 골라 쓰시오.

〈보기〉 immune   sanitary   pressure

19   _____ : the force pressing on someone or something

20   _____ : not affected by a particular disease

21   _____ : concerned with keeping things clean and healthy

Unit 07

지칭 추론

✕ 유형 소개

1. 지시대명사나 특정 명사어구가 가리키는 대상이 누구 혹은 무엇인지 묻는 문제 유형이다.
2. 지시어구가 가리키는 대상은 복잡한 개념보다는 단순히 사람이나 사물을 가리키는 경우가 대부분이다.
3. 같은 대상을 가리키더라도 지시어는 he, the man, I 등 여러 말로 등장하므로 주의해야 한다.

✕ 유형 전략

Step 1 밑줄 친 지시어는 글의 곳곳에 산재되어 있으므로 결국 글의 전체적인 내용과 문맥을 정확하게 파악해야 그 가리키는 내용도 정확하게 알 수 있다.

Step 2 한 지문에 등장하는 인물이나 사물은 많아야 3~4 가지로 제한적일 수밖에 없으므로 어떤 사람들 혹은 사물들이 등장하는지 잘 파악하면서 읽는다.

Step 3 지시어는 대개 앞에 나오는 사람, 사물을 가리키게 되어 있으므로 지시어가 가리키는 부분이 혼동될 때는 지시어 앞부분을 다시 확인한다.

Words & Phrases

actual 실제의
amazingly 놀랄 정도로, 굉장히
annual 일 년의, 일 년마다의
blank 빈, 공백의
bottom 바닥
capture 포착하다
charm 마력; 매력
critic 비평가
describe 묘사하다, 기술하다
drain 물을 빼내다
elbow 팔꿈치
encourage 용기를 돋우다, 격려하다
especially 특히
firm 굳은, 단단한

float 뜨다
fluid 유동체, 액체(기체를 포함)
liquid 액체, 유동체
location 장소, 위치
next to ~ 옆에
object 물체; 목표
ordinary 보통의
painfully 고통스럽게
pal 친구
sink 가라앉다
term 용어
terrible 끔찍한, 소름끼치는
unfamiliar 익숙하지 않은

Example

정답 및 해설 p.11

밑줄 친 ①~⑤ 중에서 가리키는 대상이 나머지 넷과 <u>다른</u> 것은?

3D printing technology has given a new life to a Canadian duckling called ① <u>Dudley</u>. He had been struggling to get by after losing a leg in a battle with a chicken. ② <u>He</u> had a hard time walking on firm ground. Determined to help ③ <u>him</u>, Doug Nelson, the owner of the duckling, went to Terence Loring, who offers 3D-printing designs. When he saw brave Dudley walking around on one leg, Terence knew he had to do something. ④ <u>He</u> spent the next few weeks creating a 3D template. When the leg and foot were finally printed and fitted on Dudley, his whole behavior changed like a charm. He shook his feathers and walked over to show the new leg off to ⑤ <u>his</u> best pal, a pig called Elsie.

✕ 문제 해결하기

Step 1 **전체적인 문맥 파악하기**
이 글은 3D 프린팅 기술로 만든 인공 다리로 새로운 삶을 살게 된 한 오리 이야기이다. 첫 문장이 주제문으로서 주제문을 보아 오리와 사람이 함께 등장할 것임을 알 수 있다.

Step 2 **등장하는 인물 혹은 사물 파악하기**
먼저 오리 Dudley가 등장하며 싸움을 한 chicken, 오리 주인 Doug Nelson, 3D 프린팅 디자이너 Terence Loring, 돼지 Elsie가 차례로 등장한다.

Step 3 **지시어 앞부분에 등장하는 인물·사물 확인하기**
②의 He 앞에 등장하는 인물 혹은 동물은 오리 Dudley뿐이므로 ①과 ②는 동일하게 오리 Dudley를 가리킨다. ④의 He 앞에는 Terence가 반복 등장하고 있다.

Step 4 **정답 확인하기**
①과 ②가 동일하게 오리를 가리키므로 ③~⑤에서 오리 아닌 다른 것을 가리키는 하나를 찾으면 된다. ④가 디자이너 Terence를 가리키므로 정답이다.

---

duckling 새끼 오리　struggle 분투하다, 투쟁하다　get by 그럭저럭 해내다, 살아남다　have a hard time -ing ~하는 데 애를 먹다　firm 굳은, 단단한　be determined to ~하기로 굳게 결심하다　template 형판, 모형　charm 마력; 매력　shake 흔들다 (shake - shook - shaken)　feather 깃털　show off 자랑하다　pal 친구

An egg sinks to the bottom if you drop ① it into a glass of ordinary drinking water but what happens if you add salt? The results are very interesting and can teach you some fun facts about density. Salt water is denser than ordinary tap water. *The denser the liquid is, the easier it is for an object to float in ② it. When you lower the egg into the liquid ③ it drops through the normal tap water until it reaches the salty water. At this point the water is dense enough for ④ it to float. If you were careful when you added the tap water to the salt water, they will not have mixed, enabling ⑤ it to float amazingly well in the middle of the glass.

1 밑줄 친 ①~⑤ 중에서 가리키는 대상이 나머지 넷과 다른 것은?

①   ②   ③   ④   ⑤

서술형
2 밑줄 친 부분을 우리말로 옮기시오.

_____

Grammar Points!   가주어 it

문장의 주어가 to부정사구일 경우 가주어 it을 문장 앞에 쓰고 to부정사구(진주어)를 뒤에 둘 수 있다. to부정사구의 의미상 주어가 있을 경우 「for + 목적격」으로 to부정사구 앞에 둔다.
The denser the liquid is, the easier **it** is <u>for an object</u> to float in it.
액체는 밀도가 높을수록 물체는 거기서 떠오르기가 더 쉽다.

sink 가라앉다 **bottom** 바닥 **ordinary** 보통의 **density** 밀도, 농도 (a. dense 밀도가 높은, 조밀한) **tap water** 수돗물 **liquid** 액체, 유동체 **object** 물체; 목표 **float** 뜨다 **lower** 떨어뜨리다, 내리다 **amazingly** 놀랄 정도로, 굉장히

Two men who were both seriously ill were in the same hospital room. ① <u>One man</u> was allowed to sit up in his bed for an hour each afternoon to help drain the fluid from his lungs. His bed was next to the room's only window. The other man had to spend all ② <u>his</u> time flat on his back. The men talked for hours. They spoke of their families, their homes, and their jobs. *Every afternoon when the man by the window could sit up, ③ <u>he</u> would describe to his roommate all the beautiful things he could see outside the window. The man in the other bed began to live for those one-hour periods. One morning, ④ <u>the man</u> by the window died. The other man moved next to the window. Painfully, he propped himself up on one elbow and looked out the window. It faced a blank wall. ⑤ <u>His roommate</u> who died had tried to encourage him.

1 밑줄 친 ①~⑤ 중에서 가리키는 대상이 나머지 넷과 <u>다른</u> 것은?

①   ②   ③   ④   ⑤

서술형

2 윗글의 내용과 일치하도록 빈칸에 적절한 말을 써넣으시오.

The man who died told _____ _____ to make his roommate happy.

Grammar Points!   과거의 습관을 나타내는 would

과거의 습관으로 '~하곤 했다'라는 의미를 나타낼 때 조동사 would를 써서 표현할 수 있다.
Every afternoon when the man by the window could sit up, he **would** describe to his roommate all the beautiful things he could see outside the window. 매일 오후, 창문 옆에 있는 남자가 앉을 수 있을 때마다 그는 자기의 병실 동료에게 그가 창문 밖으로 볼 수 있는 온갖 아름다운 것들에 대해 설명해주곤 했다.

---

seriously 심하게, 대단히   **drain** 물을 빼내다   **fluid** 유동체, 액체(기체를 포함)   **lung** 폐   **next to** ~ 옆에   **flat on one's back** 누워 있기만 하는 **describe** 묘사하다, 기술하다   **live for** ~을 사는 보람으로 삼다   **painfully** 고통스럽게   **prop** 받치다   **elbow** 팔꿈치   **blank** 빈, 공백의   **encourage** 용기를 돋우다, 격려하다

Some people travel the world without ever leaving their house; they do so by reading books about exotic locations. ① *People who are afraid to fly can nevertheless immerse themselves in a far-off place. At the end of a good travel book, ② readers can feel as if they know a place they've never visited, even if they never want to go there. Armchair travel is, in fact, less dangerous and more comfortable than actual tourism. Unfamiliar customs and food that might make ③ a traveler feel out of place actually seem very amusing to ④ them. Many people read eagerly about a traveler getting food poisoning in a strange place or sitting on a plane that nearly crashes. Then they say to themselves, "What a relief it didn't happen to ⑤ me!"

1 밑줄 친 ①~⑤ 중에서 가리키는 대상이 나머지 넷과 다른 것은?

①   ②   ③   ④   ⑤

서술형

2 글의 문맥으로 보아 밑줄 친 Armchair travel이란 무엇인지 10자 이내의 우리말로 답하시오.

_____

Grammar Points!　　관계사절의 수식에 의해 길어진 문장의 주어

주어가 관계대명사절의 수식을 받아 길어지는 경우가 있다. 이 경우 문장의 동사와 관계대명사절의 동사를 구별하는 것이 중요하다.

People who are afraid to fly can nevertheless immerse themselves in a far-off place.
비행기 타는 것을 두려워하는 사람들이라 하더라도 멀리 떨어진 장소에 자신들을 푹 빠지게 할 수 있다.

exotic 이국적인　location 장소, 위치　immerse 가라앉히다, 빠져들게 하다　far-off 멀리 떨어진　comfortable 편안한　actual 실제의　unfamiliar 익숙하지 않은　out of place 제자리를 벗어난, 곤란한　eagerly 열심히　food poisoning 식중독　crash 충돌하다, 추락하다

(A)

The Impressionists painted more wildly than traditional artists. In their paintings, (a) they tried to capture the idea of how things looked at a glance. (b) Their paintings looked a little blurry, as though they were not finished.

(B)

So, the Impressionists had (c) their own art show in 1874. There, an art critic named Louis Leroy saw Claude Monet's painting called *Impression: Sunrise*. The sun looked like a brilliant ball of orange fire in the gray sky. Mr. Leroy thought that this fiery sun was terrible.

(C)

Impressionists surprised everyone, especially the art critics who didn't like the style. *The annual art show in Paris, called the Salon, gave many (d) artists a chance to show off their paintings. Each year, a jury decided on which paintings would be displayed. The jury did not like the (e) Impressionists' work.

(D)

He thought the smoky sky and black boat were awful. He thought Monet was a bad artist. He even said that wallpaper looked better. He called this unfinished style "impressionism" and the term stuck. Thus, Impressionism was named out of dislike.

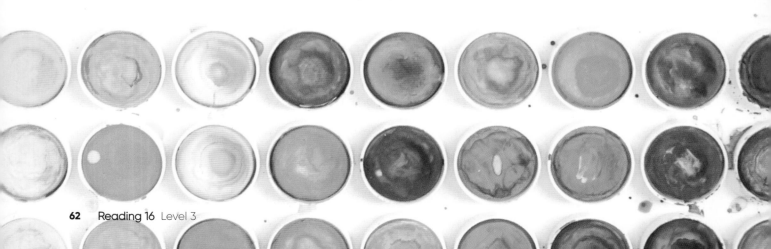

1 주어진 글 (A)에 이어질 순서로 가장 적절한 것은?

① (B) − (C) − (D)

② (B) − (D) − (C)

③ (C) − (D) − (B)

④ (C) − (B) − (D)

⑤ (D) − (B) − (C)

2 밑줄 친 (a)~(e) 중에서 가리키는 대상이 나머지 넷과 다른 것은?

① (a)　　　② (b)　　　③ (c)　　　④ (d)　　　⑤ (e)

3 윗글의 Impressionism에 관한 내용과 일치하지 않는 것은?

① 화풍을 나타내는 말이다.

② 기존 방식보다 더 거칠었다.

③ Monet의 그림에서 시작된 용어이다.

④ 출현 당시 미술계로부터 홀대받았다.

⑤ 파리의 연례 미술 전시회를 통해 처음 알려졌다.

> 서술형

4 다음 우리말과 의미가 같도록 괄호 안의 말을 알맞게 배열하시오.

그들은 그 귀여운 개를 Rover라고 불렀다. (dog, Rover, the, they, called, cute)

_____

Grammar Points! 　삽입어구

문장 중에 독립적으로 삽입되어 설명이나 주석을 다는 역할을 한다. 일반적으로 삽입어구 앞뒤로 콤마(,)나 대시(—)를 둔다.

The annual art show in Paris, **called the Salon,** gave many artists a chance to show off their paintings. Salon이라 불렸던 파리의 연례 미술 전시회는 많은 화가에게 그림을 자랑할 기회를 주었다.

Impressionist 인상파 화가(Impressionism 인상파)　wildly 거칠게　capture 포착하다　at a glance 한눈에, 잠깐 보아서　blurry 흐릿한　critic 비평가
fiery 불타는 듯한, 불의　terrible 끔찍한, 소름끼치는　especially 특히　annual 일 년의, 일 년마다의　jury 배심원, 심사원　display 전시하다　smoky
연기 나는, 연기와 같은　awful 무서운, 끔찍한　term 용어　stick 들러붙다, 움직이지 않게 되다

Word Check ✕ ✕ ✕

정답 및 해설 p.12

[1-10] 영어는 우리말로, 우리말은 영어로 나타내시오.

1 firm : _____

2 fluid : _____

3 crash : _____

4 ordinary : _____

5 especially : _____

6 물체, 목표 : _____

7 밀도가 높은 : _____

8 끔찍한, 소름끼치는 : _____

9 뜨다 : _____

10 분투하다 : _____

[11-13] 괄호 안에서 알맞은 말을 고르시오.

11 The drawer (stuck / stirred) and would not open.

12 They had to (fill / fit) the idea to their philosophy.

13 What is his (awfully / annual) income?

[14-16] 빈칸에 들어갈 말을 〈보기〉에서 골라 알맞은 형태로 쓰시오.

> 〈보기〉 show   describe   blurry

14 My grandpa _____ the horrors of war in great detail.

15 The trees were just _____ shapes.

16 Young parents love _____ off their new baby.

17 **밑줄 친 부분에 올 수 없는 말을 고르시오.**

> He taught in a(n) _____ style.

① amusing   ② strange   ③ blank   ④ unfamiliar

[18-20] 다음의 뜻에 해당하는 단어를 〈보기〉에서 골라 쓰시오.

> 〈보기〉 jury   immerse   exotic

18 _____ : a panel of judges

19 _____ : from another part of the world, excitingly strange

20 _____ : to cover completely in a liquid

Unit 08

심경 · 분위기 추론

✕ 유형 소개

1. 글쓴이나 글에 등장하는 인물이 어떤 감정이나 태도를 갖고 있는지, 글에서 묘사하고 있는 분위기는 어떠한지 파악하는 유형이다.
2. 감정이나 분위기를 나타내는 단어가 직접적으로 제시되어 있기도 하고 글 이면에 숨어 있기도 하므로 드러나 있는 단서들을 통해 추론하는 능력이 필요하다.
3. 설명문이나 논설문이 아닌 소설이나 수필 같은 문학 작품의 일부분으로서 특정 상황을 묘사하는 글에서 주로 출제된다.

✕ 유형 전략

Step 1 글의 도입부를 읽고 인물, 시간, 장소 등 묘사하고 있는 상황이나 사건의 배경 정보를 파악한다.

Step 2 태도나 심경, 분위기를 나타내는 특정 어구들에 주목한다. 주로 형용사나 부사, 감정을 나타내는 동사들이 해당된다.

Step 3 등장인물이 하는 동작이나 행동, 글의 상황을 나타내는 어구 뒤에 감추어진 뜻이나 행간을 읽어야 한다. 단편적인 내용에 치중하지 말고 글을 끝까지 읽은 후 종합적으로 판단하는 것이 중요하다.

Words & Phrases

admission 입학(허가)	**pine** 소나무
aroma 향기	**position** (~에) 두다; 자리를 잡다
blow (바람이) 불다	**process** 과정
bow 절하다	**puzzle** 당황하게 하다
continually 계속해서	**shade** 그늘
criminal 범죄의	**stain** 얼룩
define 규정짓다, 정의하다	**stern** 엄한, 엄격한 (= strict)
deposit (특정 장소에) 놓다, 맡기다	**stretch** 뻗어 있다, 펼쳐져 있다
heritage 유산, 물려받은 것	**stuff** 채워 넣다
impatient 참을성 없는	**suspect** 의심하다
journey 여행하다	**uncertain** 불확실한
massive 대량의, 육중한	**visible** 볼 수 있는

Example

다음 글에 드러난 주인공의 심경으로 가장 적절한 것은?

Every day at 5:00 p.m., instead of playing with our fourth- and fifth-grade friends or sneaking out to the empty lot to hunt ghosts and animal bones, my brother and I had to go to Chinese school. No amount of kicking, screaming, or pleading could dissuade my mother, who was solidly determined to have us learn the language of our heritage. Forcibly, she walked us the seven long, hilly blocks from our home to school, depositing our defiant, tearful faces before the stern principal. My only memory of him is that he swayed on his heels like a palm tree and he always clasped his impatient, twitching hands behind his back. I thought him a crazy child killer, and that if we ever saw his hands, we'd be in big trouble.

① excited and thrilled

② reluctant and scared

③ regretful and ashamed

④ proud and delighted

⑤ bored and exhausted

✕ 문제 해결하기

Step 1 **글의 도입부를 통해 인물, 사건의 배경 정보 파악하기**
첫 문장을 통해 주인공(I)은 매일 방과 후에 친구들과 놀지 못하고 중국어 학교에 가야 하는 상황에 처해 있음을 알 수 있다.

Step 2 **태도, 심경, 분위기를 나타내는 특정 어구들에 주목하기**
등장인물들을 묘사하고 있는 단어에 밑줄을 그으면서 글을 읽어 나간다.
(1) my brother and I: kicking, screaming, pleading, defiant, tearful faces
(2) my mother: solidly determined, forcibly
(3) principal: stern, swayed on his heels like a palm tree, clasped his impatient, twitching hand behind his back, a crazy child killer

Step 3 **상황과 단서들을 통해 인물의 심경을 종합적으로 판단하기**
주인공(I)이 엄마에게 한 행동들을 묘사하는 단어를 통해 중국어 학교에 가는 것을 몹시 싫어했다는 것을 알 수 있으며 중국어 학교 교장 선생님을 묘사한 단어들을 통해 선생님을 두려워했음을 알 수 있다. 이를 잘 나타낸 선택지를 고른다.

---

sneak out 몰래 나가다 lot 한 구획의 땅 no amount of 아무리 많은 ~도 …않다 plead 간청하다 dissuade ~를 설득하여 단념시키다 (↔ persuade)
solidly 단호하게, 굳게 heritage 유산, 물려받은 것 forcibly 강제로 deposit (특정 장소에) 놓다, 맡기다 defiant 반항적인 stern 엄한, 엄격한
(= strict) sway 흔들리다, 한쪽으로 기울다 palm 야자, 종려나무 clasp 손을 꽉 잡다 impatient 참을성 없는 twitch (근육 등이) 씰룩거리다

I was a junior in high school, deeply immersed in the college admissions process. The future stretched out before me in an endless red carpet. Just two blocks away from my high school, my grandmother lay in her hospital bed. Her cancer had moved into her bones. Her pain was so fierce that no amount of a strong painkiller could take it away. Those two blocks felt like the longest in the world. *After school, I used to journey alone from a world defined by the future to a world that had no future. What would I say to Grandma? How could I tell her that I was making plans for later, for what I would be doing once she was no longer here? Better to sit silently than speak of the future we wouldn't share.

1 방과 후에 할머니를 방문할 때 필자의 심경의 변화로 가장 적절한 것은?

① nervous → relieved
② disappointed → amused
③ enthusiastic → hopeless
④ confused → curious
⑤ comfortable → indifferent

서술형

2 필자가 할머니에게 아무 말도 할 수 없었던 이유가 무엇인지 우리말로 쓰시오.

_____

Grammar Points! 조동사 used to의 용법

'~하곤 했다'는 의미로 과거 습관을 나타낼 때 조동사 used to를 쓸 수 있다. 이때 동작이나 행동을 나타내므로 같은 의미의 would 를 쓸 수도 있다.

After school, I **used to** journey alone from a world defined by the future to a world that had no future. 방과 후 나는 미래에 의해 규정지어진 세계에서 미래가 전혀 없는 세계로 혼자 여행을 하곤 했다. – 과거의 습관

junior (3년제의) 2학년생 (cf. freshman 1학년) immerse 몰두하게 하다, 빠져들게 하다 admission 입학(허가) process 과정 stretch 뻗어 있다, 펼쳐져 있다 endless 끝없는 fierce 몹시 사나운, 격심한 take away 제거하다, 없애다 journey 여행하다 define 규정짓다, 정의하다

The smell and sound of oak trees and pine trees at the start of the trail gets visitors excited for the journey. The sun hitting the trees makes the air fresh with a leafy aroma. Overhead, the wind blows through the leaves, making a soft noise. <u>Closer to the waterfall</u>, the shade from the tall oak trees and short pine trees creates a shielding blanket. When the sun comes out, it fills the area with light, showing the vapor coming off of the trees and plants. *To the left of the trail are rocks that are positioned perfectly for viewing the waterfall. Water splashes as it hits the rocks. To one side, a big rock with a sign describes how the waterfalls were formed. The waterfall itself is beautiful, like looking through a transparent, sparkling window of diamonds. The water is so clear that objects on the other side are visible. It is like a never-ending stream of water that splashes onto rocks.

1 윗글에 드러난 분위기로 가장 적절한 것은?

① lively and splendid   ② noisy and busy

③ fearful and frightening   ④ gloomy and spooky

⑤ drowsy and monotonous

서술형

2 밑줄 친 **Closer to the waterfall**을 주어와 동사를 포함한 절로 바꾸어 쓰시오.

Grammar Points! 부사구 도치 구문

장소나 방향을 나타내는 부사구가 문장 앞으로 나오면 이어지는 주어와 동사의 위치가 대개 도치되는 것에 주의한다.

To the left of the trail <u>are rocks</u> that are positioned perfectly for viewing the waterfall.
오솔길 왼쪽에는 폭포를 보기에 완벽하게 좋은 위치에 자리 잡은 바위들이 있다.

---

pine 소나무 **trail** 오솔길 **leafy** 잎이 우거진, 잎으로 된 **aroma** 향기 **blow** (바람이) 불다 **waterfall** 폭포 **shade** 그늘 **shield** 감싸다, 보호하다 **blanket** 담요 **vapor** 증기, 수증기 **position** (~에) 두다; 자리를 잡다 **splash** (물 등을) 튀기다 **sign** 표지 **transparent** 투명한 **sparkling** 반짝이는, 거품이 이는 **visible** 볼 수 있는

"Beautiful! Beautiful! The old guaiacum test was very clumsy and uncertain. So is the microscopic examination for blood corpuscles. The latter is valueless if the stains are a few hours old. *Now, this appears to act as well whether the blood is old or new. If this test had been invented, hundreds of men who are now walking the earth would have paid the penalty of their crimes long ago." "Indeed!" I murmured. "Criminal cases are continually based upon that one point. A man is suspected of a crime months perhaps after it has been committed. His clothes are examined, and brownish stains discovered upon them. Are they blood stains, or mud stains, or rust stains, or fruit stains, or what are they? That is a question which has puzzled many an expert, and why? Because there was no reliable test. Now we have the Sherlock Holmes' test, and there will no longer be any difficulty." The eyes of Sherlock Holmes fairly glittered as he spoke, and he put his hand over his heart and bowed as if to some applauding crowd his imagination created.

* guaiacum 유창목 기름

1 윗글에 드러난 he의 심경으로 가장 적절한 것은??
① afraid and sorry
② embarrassed and annoyed
③ concerned and nervous
④ amazed and confused
⑤ proud and excited

서술형
2 밑줄 친 문장을 다음 주어진 말로 시작하여 고쳐 쓰시오.

The microscopic examination for blood corpuscles _____

_____ .

Grammar Points! 접속사 whether

whether는 명사절을 이끌어 '~인지 아닌지'란 뜻으로 쓰이지만 '~이든 아니든'이란 의미의 양보 부사절을 이끌기도 한다.
Now, this appears to act as well **whether** the blood is old or new.
지금 이것은 피가 오래되었든 새것이든 상관없이 작용하는 것 같아. – 양보 부사절

clumsy 솜씨 없는, 서투른 uncertain 불확실한 microscopic 현미경의 corpuscle 소체, 혈구 stain 얼룩 appear (to-v) ~인 것 같다 murmur 중얼거리다 criminal 범죄의 continually 계속해서 suspect 의심하다 commit 죄를 범하다 brownish 갈색을 띤 rust 녹 puzzle 당황하게 하다 reliable 신뢰할 수 있는 glitter 반짝이다, 빛나다 bow 절하다 applaud 갈채를 보내다

*I don't believe that it's the fear of illness that casts a dark shadow over the future of people in my age group. We can deal with illness, even an illness that requires massive doses of chemicals to treat it. No, it's _____ that terrorizes our four o'clock mornings.

I've tried to convince myself that <u>it</u> won't happen to me. The fear that hangs over my circle of friends will never be mine. Then I talk with my mother, who at 95 is in an assisted living facility in California, thousands of miles away. She has trouble holding onto a thought for 20 minutes. Our nightly phone calls seem to travel in circles, the same question constantly resurfacing, followed by the same answers.

I tell her not to worry about her memory. After all, she has ninety-five years of memories stuffed inside her head. She has to do periodic housecleaning <u>in order to let others in</u>. She always laughs when I tell her this. Then she asks me how my grandchildren are, the question that had just been answered a moment ago. Maybe I call her too often. Maybe I should give her some time to build some different memories. I don't know. All I know is that I have to call her. I have to hear the same questions and give the same answers, day in, day out.

1 윗글의 빈칸에 들어갈 말로 가장 적절한 것은?

① the damaged family relationship

② the fear of sleeplessness

③ the severe pain inside our bodies

④ the anxiety about an uncertain future

⑤ the loss of our memories and our dignity

2 윗글에 드러난 I의 심경으로 가장 적절한 것은?

① confused and embarrassed

② amused and delighted

③ concerned and nervous

④ confident and determined

⑤ helpless and desperate

서술형
3 밑줄 친 it이 가리키는 내용을 우리말로 쓰시오.

_____

서술형
4 밑줄 친 in order to let others in을 다음 주어진 말로 시작하는 절로 바꾸어 쓰시오.

so that _____

Grammar Points! 〈It is[was] ~ that ...〉 강조 구문

문장의 주어, 목적어, 부사어구를 강조할 경우 「It is[was] ~ that ...」을 이용할 수 있다.
I don't believe that **it's the fear of illness that** casts a dark shadow over the future of people in my age group. 나는 내 나이 또래 사람들의 미래에 먹구름을 드리우는 것은 병에 대한 두려움이 아니라고 생각한다.

---

cast a dark shadow 먹구름을 드리우다   deal with 다루다, 처리하다   massive 대량의, 육중한   dose (약의 1회) 복용량   terrorize ~을 무섭게 하다
convince ~에게 확신시키다   hang over (위험 등이) ~에 다가와 있다, (절망 등이) ~을 괴롭히다   assisted living facility 양로원   constantly 끊임없이
resurface 다시 떠오르다   stuff 채워 넣다   periodic 주기적인, 정기의   day in, day out 매일매일

Word Check ✕ ✕ ✕

정답 및 해설 p.14

[1-10] 영어는 우리말로, 우리말은 영어로 나타내시오.

1 solidly : _____

2 murmur : _____

3 terrorize : _____

4 stain : _____

5 vapor : _____

6 신뢰할 수 있는 : _____

7 갈채를 보내다 : _____

8 진통제 : _____

9 오솔길 : _____

10 입학(허가) : _____

[11-13] 괄호 안에서 알맞은 말을 고르시오.

11 The ozone layer (shades / shields) the Earth from the Sun's ultraviolet rays.

12 They were going to set off in the storm, but were (dissuaded / pleaded).

13 She (defined / deposited) a pile of reports on my desk.

[14-16] 빈칸에 들어갈 말을 〈보기〉에서 골라 알맞은 형태로 쓰시오.

〈보기〉 commit   convince   puzzle

14 People _____ suicide because of lack of control over their life.

15 I was _____ by his sudden change of attitude.

16 Everybody is an expert and it is difficult to _____ them.

[17-19] 짝지어진 단어의 관계가 같도록 빈칸에 알맞은 말을 쓰시오.

17 help : assist = strict : _____

18 certain : uncertain = patient : _____

19 crime : criminal = period : _____

[20-22] 다음의 뜻에 해당하는 단어를 〈보기〉에서 골라 쓰시오.

〈보기〉 clumsy   principal   transparent

20 _____ : being able to see through something

21 _____ : the head of a school

22 _____ : not skillful, handling things in a careless way

Unit 09

내용 일치

⚹ 유형 소개

1. 글을 읽고 세부정보를 바르게 파악할 수 있는지 확인하는 유형이다.
2. 주어진 글을 읽고 선택지 중 글의 내용과 일치하거나 일치하지 않는 설명을 고르는 문제이다.
3. 선택지 내용의 진위를 주어진 글에 국한되어 판단해야 하는 유형이다.

⚹ 유형 전략

Step 1 글의 대략적인 주제를 빠르게 파악하면서 글 전체를 비교적 꼼꼼하게 읽는다.

Step 2 중요 세부사항이나 숫자가 나오는 부분은 일단 밑줄을 치면서 읽는다.

Step 3 선택지를 주의 깊게 읽는다. 상식엔 맞지만 글의 내용과 다르거나 글에 나온 사실이나 표현을 일부 섞어 교묘하게 만든 오답에 특히 주의해야 한다.

Words & Phrases

account for (비율을) 차지하다, ~을 설명하다
average 일반적인, 평균의
cell 세포
cheap 값싼 (↔ expensive 값비싼)
chemical 화학 물질, 화학의
consume 소비하다
continent 대륙
contrary to ~와는 반대로
deliver 배달하다
discovery 발견
environment 환경
extension 연장
figure out 산정하다, 이해하다
garbage 쓰레기
irresponsible 무책임한

lawn 잔디
limited 한정된
myth 신화, 근거 없는 생각
nutrient 영양소
pamphlet 소책자
poison 독
popularity 인기 (*a.* popular 인기 있는)
refer to ~을 가리키다
require 요구하다
sticky 끈적거리는 (*v.* stick 달라붙다)
tough 힘든, 거친
trap 덫으로 잡다; 덫
uncontrollable 제어할 수 없는
underground 지하에서; 지하의; 지하

Example

natural resources에 관한 다음 글의 내용과 일치하지 <u>않는</u> 것은?

Although the U.S. accounts for less than 5 percent of the world's population, it uses 25 percent of the world's natural resources. One of the worst examples of waste is the amount of gasoline we consume. The popularity of sport utility vehicles (SUVs) has dramatically increased gasoline consumption. SUVs are said to use 25 percent more gasoline per mile than the average car. We also waste water by using excessive amounts of water while we wash dishes, brush our teeth, take showers, water lawns, and do other chores. We must stop our excessive use of limited resources.

① 미국은 전 세계 천연자원의 1/4을 사용한다.
② 미국의 가솔린 소비는 낭비가 가장 심각한 천연자원에 속한다.
③ SUV는 다른 일반 차량에 비해 기름을 많이 사용한다.
④ 가정 용수는 용도는 다양하지만 낭비는 심하지 않다.
⑤ 가솔린이나 물은 양이 한정되어 있는 천연자원이다.

✕ 문제 해결하기

Step 1 주제를 염두에 두면서 꼼꼼하게 읽기
마지막 문장이 주제문이지만 첫 문장부터 과도한 천연자원 사용 문제를 끌어오고 있으므로 이어질 내용에 대해 예측하며 중요 세부사항을 꼼꼼하게 읽는다.

Step 2 중요 세부사항에 밑줄 치기
주제와 문제 형식을 보아 어떤 자원이 얼마만 한 양으로, 누구에 의해서 어떻게 낭비되는지가 중요할 것이므로 the U.S., 25 percent of the world's natural resources, The popularity of sport utility vehicles, 25 percent more gasoline 등에 밑줄을 긋는다.

Step 3 선택지를 주의 깊게 읽기
본문에서 가정 용수의 여러 용도를 언급했지만 낭비가 심하지 않다고 언급한 바는 없으므로 ④는 틀린 내용이다. 이렇게 일부는 일치하지만 일부는 일치하지 않는 선택지에 특히 주의해야 한다.

account for (비율을) 차지하다, ~을 설명하다 natural resources 천연자원 consume 소비하다 popularity 인기 (a. popular 인기 있는) vehicle 탈것 (Sport Utility Vehicle 스포츠 활동에 적합한 차량, SUV) dramatically 극적으로, 눈부시게 average 일반적인, 평균의 lawn 잔디 chore 허드렛일, 집안일 limited 한정된

*In Antarctica, you learn not to take anything for granted – not water, food, or even energy. Everything people depend on has to be shipped or flown into the continent. All fuel and supplies must be delivered during the short Antarctic summer. Nothing comes in or goes out during the long, dark Antarctic winter. As for drinking water, special systems and a great deal of energy are needed to take salt out of seawater. Every bit of garbage a person might produce in a day has to be transported off the continent to protect the Antarctic environment. To live and work at the bottom of the world, <u>whether you are there to study penguins or bake bread,</u> requires very careful planning.

1 Antarctica에서의 생활에 관한 윗글의 내용과 일치하는 것은?

① 배나 비행기로 생활물자를 공급받는다.
② 과학 연구원들만 살고 있다.
③ 겨울엔 육지로부터 최소한의 생활 물자만 공급된다.
④ 환경보호를 위해 쓰레기 자연분해 시스템이 갖춰져 있다.
⑤ 눈이나 빙하를 정화하여 마시는 물로 사용한다.

서술형
2 밑줄 친 부분을 우리말로 옮기시오.

_____

Grammar Points!　　**to부정사의 부정**

to부정사의 내용을 not/never로 부정할 경우 부정어 not/never를 to부정사 바로 앞에 놓는다.
In Antarctica, you learn **not to take** anything for granted – not water, food, or even energy.
남극에서 당신은 물, 음식, 심지어 에너지조차 어떤 것도 당연한 일로 생각하지 않는 것을 배우게 된다.

Antarctica 남극 대륙 (Antarctic 남극 지방의 ↔ Arctic 북극 지방의)　take ~ for granted ~를 당연시하다　continent 대륙　fuel 연료　deliver 배달하다　a great deal of 많은　garbage 쓰레기　transport 수송하다 (trans(= across)+port(운반하다))　environment 환경　require 요구하다

*Some pamphlets published in England in the early nineteenth century suggest women who drank tea were viewed as irresponsible as whisky drinkers in Ireland. Critics saw the practice of tea drinking as thoughtless and uncontrollable. They thought women who drank tea wasted their time and money, drawing themselves away from their duty to care for their husbands and home. There was also a myth about tea having drug-like qualities, as it was still a mysterious substance from China. People thought that tea became addictive over time. Moreover, tea was not as cheap _____ it is today, and was considered a luxury for poor women to enjoy.

1 19세기 Ireland의 tea drinking에 관한 윗글의 내용과 일치하지 <u>않는</u> 것은?

① 음주에 버금가는 부정적인 행위로 간주됐다.
② 차를 마시는 여성은 가정에 소홀하다고 여겨졌다.
③ 마약처럼 중독성이 있는 것으로 간주됐다.
④ 남성들보다 여성들이 주로 차를 마셨다.
⑤ 당시의 차는 가격이 비싸서 사치품으로 여겨졌다.

서술형

2 빈칸에 알맞은 한 단어를 윗글에서 찾아 쓰시오.

_____

Grammar Points! 동등 비교

두 개의 정도가 같음을 나타낼 때 『as + 형용사/부사 + as ~』의 형태로 '~와 같은 정도로 (형용사/부사)하다'는 뜻을 표현한다.
Some pamphlets published in England in the early nineteenth century suggest women who drank tea were viewed **as irresponsible as** whisky drinkers in Ireland. 19세기 초 영국에서 출판된 소책자에 의하면 아일랜드에서는 차를 마시는 여자는 위스키를 마시는 사람만큼이나 무책임한 것으로 보였던 것 같다.

---

pamphlet 소책자 **publish** 출판하다 **irresponsible** 무책임한 **practice** 행위, 습관 **thoughtless** 분별없는, 무심한 **uncontrollable** 제어할 수 없는 **myth** 신화, 근거 없는 생각 **quality** 특성, 질 **mysterious** 불가사의한 **addictive** 중독성의 (v. addict 중독되게 하다) **luxury** 사치품

Scientists discovered a plant in Brazil that eats worms! It was tricky for scientists to even make this discovery because the plant, called Philcoxia, traps its prey underground. Most of its leaves are actually underground and the leaves are very sticky – sticky enough to trap tiny worms called nematodes. There are not a lot of other nutrients around in the sandy, rocky, dry area where Philcoxia lives. Tough conditions are true for other meat-eating plants, but *Philcoxia is the first plant we know of to trap its prey underground. Now that we know meat-eating plants can be found underground, it is quite possible that there are more of them in existence than we first thought.

* nematode 선충류

1 Philcoxia에 관한 윗글의 내용과 일치하지 <u>않는</u> 것은?

① 브라질에서 볼 수 있는 식물이다.

② 대부분의 잎이 땅 밑에 있다.

③ 영양분이 많지 않은 토양에서 자란다.

④ 끈적이는 잎이 벌레를 잡는 수단이다.

⑤ 최초로 알려진 육식 식물이다.

서술형

2 윗글로 보아 육식 식물의 공통적인 생육환경은 무엇인지 10자 내외의 우리말로 쓰시오.

_____

Grammar Points! 명사구를 수식하는 어구들의 수

명사구를 수식하는 어구들이 반드시 한 개만 있는 것은 아니다. 두 개 이상의 어구가 한 명사구를 수식할 수 있음에 유의해야 한다.

Philcoxia is **the first plant** we know of to trap its prey underground.

필콕시아는 지하에서 먹이를 잡는 것으로 우리가 알고 있는 최초의 식물이다.

tricky 다루기 힘든, 교묘한 discovery 발견 trap 덫으로 잡다; 덫 prey 먹이 underground 지하에서; 지하의; 지하 sticky 끈적거리는 (v. stick 달라 붙다) nutrient 영양소 tough 힘든, 거친 quite 훨씬, 꽤 existence 존재, 실존

(A)

Glow-in-the-dark cats? It may sound like science fiction, but they've been around for years. Cabbages that produce scorpion poison? It's been done. *Oh, and the next time you need a vaccine, the doctor might just give you a banana. All these strange things are possible thanks to genetic engineering.

(B)

Unfortunately, these artificial genes may one day be added routinely. Novel organisms bring novel risks, however, as well as the desired effects. These risks must be carefully figured out because all effects must be good for us.

(C)

It refers to a set of technologies that are used to change the genetic makeup of cells. The technologies can also move genes across the boundaries of various species. Those techniques are highly advanced because they handle genetic material and other important chemicals.

(D)

Therefore, contrary to the arguments made by some proponents, it is far from being a minor extension of existing technologies. It is a new technology that creates artificial novel genes.

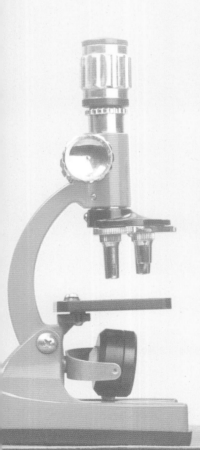

1 주어진 글 (A)에 이어질 내용을 순서에 맞게 배열한 것으로 가장 적절한 것은?

① (B) − (C) − (D)　　　② (B) − (D) − (C)　　　③ (C) − (D) − (B)

④ (C) − (B) − (D)　　　⑤ (D) − (B) − (C)

2 윗글의 요지로 가장 적절한 것은?

① 유전자 공학은 활용범위가 무궁무진하다.

② 유전자 공학 기술은 신중하게 사용되어야 한다.

③ 유전자 공학은 개발이 전면 중지되어야 한다.

④ 유전자 공학은 매우 정교한 기술의 집합체이다.

⑤ 유전자 조작 식품은 인간의 건강을 해친다.

3 genetic engineering에 관한 윗글의 내용과 일치하지 <u>않는</u> 것은?

① 세포의 유전자 구성을 인위적으로 바꾸는 기술이다.

② 동물의 성질을 식물에 옮겨 놓을 수도 있다.

③ 인간에게 필요한 생물학적 자원을 손쉽게 제공할 수 있다.

④ 예기치 않은 결과를 가져올 수 있다.

⑤ 옹호론자들은 기존 기술과는 근본적으로 다른 기술로 본다.

서술형

4 밑줄 친 문장을 다음과 같이 바꿀 때 빈칸에 알맞은 말을 써넣으시오.

Novel organisms bring ＿＿＿＿＿＿ ＿＿＿＿＿＿ the desired effects, however, ＿＿＿＿＿＿
＿＿＿＿＿＿ novel risks.

Grammar Points!　시간, 조건을 나타내는 부사절의 시제

시간이나 조건을 나타내는 부사절에서는 현재 시제로 미래를 표현한다.

Oh, and the next time you need a vaccine, the doctor might just give you a banana.

아, 그리고 다음에 당신이 백신이 필요하다고 한다면 의사는 그저 바나나를 줄지도 모른다.

glow-in-the-dark 야광의 (v. glow 빛나다)　scorpion 전갈　poison 독　genetic engineering 유전자 공학　routinely 일상적으로 (a. routine 일상적인)　organism 유기체, 생물　desired 바라던, 훌륭한　figure out 산정하다. 이해하다　makeup 구성. 구조　cell 세포　species 종(생물 분류의 기초 단위)　material 물질　chemical 화학 물질. 화학의　contrary to ~와는 반대로　proponent 찬성자 (↔ opponent 반대자)　extension 연장

Word Check ✕ ✕ ✕

정답 및 해설 p.15

[1-10] 영어는 우리말로, 우리말은 영어로 나타내시오.

1 cheap : _____

2 extension : _____

3 publish : _____

4 prey : _____

5 species : _____

6 집안일, 허드렛일 : _____

7 중독성의 : _____

8 인공의 : _____

9 수송하다 : _____

10 대륙 : _____

[11-13] 괄호 안에서 알맞은 말을 고르시오.

11 How can we find out which plants contain a particular (medical / chemical)?

12 There's a (common / routine) check of passports at the gate.

13 Attendance (accounts / publishes) for ten percent of the grade.

[14-16] 빈칸에 들어갈 말을 〈보기〉에서 골라 알맞은 형태로 쓰시오.

〈보기〉 granted   discover   require

14 Students are _____ to attend classes.

15 Several new species of plants have been _____.

16 I guess that I take a lot of things for _____.

[17-18] 다음 짝지어진 단어의 관계가 같도록 빈칸에 알맞은 말을 쓰시오.

17 regular : irregular = expensive : _____

18 novel : new = trash : _____

[19-21] 다음의 뜻에 해당하는 단어를 〈보기〉에서 골라 쓰시오.

〈보기〉 proponent   substance   sticky

19 _____ : tending to attach because of a glue-like surface

20 _____ : a person who argues in favour of something

21 _____ : that which has mass and occupies space, a material

80 Reading 16 *Level 3*

Unit
10

함축 의미
추론

✕ 유형 소개

1. 두 가지 이상의 뜻으로 해석될 수 있는 어구 혹은 비유적 의미를 담고 있는 어구에 밑줄을 그어 놓고 그것이 구체적으로 뜻하는 것이 무엇인지 묻는 유형이다.
2. 문자 그대로의 의미가 아닌, 함축되어 있는 의미를 추론해야 하므로 글 전체의 맥락 속에서 판단해야 한다.
3. 다양한 종류의 글에서 출제될 수 있으며 다의어나 구어, 숙어 표현들을 잘 알아두는 것이 도움이 된다.

✕ 유형 전략

Step 1 ▶ 문자적 뜻만으로는 정답을 찾을 수 없다. 반드시 글의 큰 흐름 안에서 글의 주제나 요지에 의거하여 밑줄 친 부분이 실제로 의미하는 바를 생각해 보아야 한다.

Step 2 ▶ 인물들이 등장하는 경우 그들이 처한 상황 속에서 각자 한 말을 비교해 보고 밑줄 친 부분이 어떤 함축 의미를 지닐 수 있는지 생각해 보아야 한다.

Step 3 ▶ 밑줄 친 어구에는 여러 가지 의미로 쓰이는 다의어, 앞서 언급된 내용이나 추상적인 상황을 가리키는 대명사, 문자적 의미와는 전혀 다른 뜻을 가지고 있는 숙어나 구어 표현 등이 자주 등장한다. 평소에 이런 표현들을 잘 익혀두도록 하자.

Words & Phrases

altogether 완전히
attack 공격하다
attempt 시도; 시도하다
available 이용 가능한
bounce off 튕기다
degree 정도, (각도의 단위인) 도
diet 식품, 식이요법
disappointed 실망한
eager 열망하는, 열심인(= anxious)
envious 시기하는(v. envy 시기하다)
experiment 실험, 실험하다
fortunate 운 좋은
insert 넣다, 끼우다

marine 바다의, 해양의
medical 의학의
partition 분할, 구획
press 누르다
raw 날것의
recommend 추천하다, 권하다
remove 제거하다
self-esteem 자기 존중
separate 분리된 (= divided)
share 공유하다
store 저장하다
take one's place 자리를 대신하다
varying 다양한; 변하는

Example

밑줄 친 부분의 의미를 an old lady가 이해한 바로 가장 잘 나타낸 것은?

Doctors often work in the same offices and share the services of one or more receptionists. These workers are told never to recommend one doctor over another. They simply tell patients a doctor who has time available.

One day an old lady asked the receptionist in a soft voice, "Can you please tell me who is the best doctor for me?" She didn't want to break the rules and answered the patient kindly, "Oh, I'm sorry, ma'am, but I can't recommend any of our doctors."

"Well, I guess you know best," said the disappointed woman, as she left the medical office to look for a good doctor.

① 현재 진료 가능한 의사가 아무도 없습니다.
② 추천해줄 만한 훌륭한 의사는 아무도 없습니다.
③ 잠시 기다리시면 의사를 추천해드리겠습니다.
④ 제가 특정 의사를 추천해드릴 순 없습니다.
⑤ 당신의 병을 치료해 줄 의사는 없습니다.

✕ 문제 해결하기

Step 1 주제나 요지 등 글의 큰 흐름을 파악하기
특정 의사를 추천해서는 안 된다는 규정이 있는 병원의 receptionist에게 고객(an old lady)이 찾아와 어떤 의사가 가장 훌륭한지 묻고 있는 상황이다.

Step 2 등장인물들이 처한 상황을 통해 밑줄 친 부분의 함축 의미 파악하기
밑줄 친 부분을 말한 receptionist는 규정 때문에 추천해줄 수 없다고 얘기한 것이지만 an old lady의 응답을 보면 그 말을 다른 식으로 이해했음을 알 수 있다. 여성이 밑줄 친 말을 어떻게 이해했는지 알기 위한 결정적 단서는 she left the medical office to look for a good doctor.라는 부분에서 알 수 있다.

share 공유하다 receptionist 접수원 (v. receive 받다 / n. reception 수납, 접수) recommend 추천하다, 권하다 patient 환자 available 이용 가능한 break rules 규칙을 어기다 disappointed 실망한 medical 의학의 look for ~을 찾다

A lot of people talk about "going green," but I am living a true green lifestyle. After feeling regret about eating two cinnamon buns at breakfast one morning, I decided to stick to a new, green diet. My diet is filled with farm-fresh spinach, asparagus, peas, green beans and other dark, leafy vegetables. I'm eating so many of these greens that I hope my arteries won't beg for mercy, claiming they just can't store any more vitamin A. I am chewing so many raw carrots I fear the whites of my eyes will turn orange. Unfortunately, <u>while I am eager to go green, my family is seeing red.</u> "Brown rice and vegetables again?" *one of my four kids asked angrily after being given three straight meals without meat or bread. As an adolescent, he considers <u>it</u> his job not to like anything.

* artery 동맥

1 밑줄 친 부분이 의미하는 바를 가장 잘 나타낸 것은?

① 채식으로 인해 가족들의 건강이 좋아지고 있다.
② 가족들은 채식 식단에 화를 내고 있다.
③ 가족들도 친환경적인 생활을 위해 노력하고 있다.
④ 나는 육식을 하지만 가족들은 채식을 고집하고 있다.
⑤ 가족들은 채식의 효과에 확신을 표하고 있다.

[서술형]
2 밑줄 친 it이 가리키는 내용을 찾아 쓰시오.

_____

Grammar Points!   **동명사의 수동태**

'~되는 것'이라는 뜻의 동명사 수동태는 『being p.p.』로 나타낸다.
One of my four kids asked angrily after **being given** three straight meals without meat or bread.
세 끼니가 연속으로 고기나 빵 없이 주어진 후에 네 아이들 중 한 명이 화를 내며 물었다.

---

go green 친환경적으로 되다   **feel regret** 후회하다   **cinnamon** 시나몬, 계피   **bun** (작고 둥글납작한) 빵   **stick to** ~을 고수하다   **diet** 식품, 식이요법
farm-fresh 농장 직송의   **spinach** 시금치   **beg for mercy** 자비를 빌다   **store** 저장하다   **raw** 날것의   **eager** 열망하는, 열심인(= anxious)   **see red**
몹시 화를 내다   **brown rice** 현미   **adolescent** 청소년

Mr. Lewis was a dance teacher. *He was a nice man and always had a lot of students who did come to his classes every week. One year he moved to a new town and was soon teaching many students in the dance school there, but then he decided to move again to a big city where he would have more work. When one of the ladies who regularly came to his classes heard that he was going to leave, she said to him, "The teacher who takes your place won't be as good as you are." Mr. Lewis was happy when he heard this, but he said, "Oh, no! I'm sure he'll be as good as I am – or ⓐ even better." The lady said, "No. Five teachers have come and gone while I've been here, and each new one was worse than the last."

1 밑줄 친 부분이 의미하는 바로 가장 적절한 것은?

① Lewis 선생의 춤 실력은 대단하다.

② 처음보다는 마지막에 춤을 추는 것이 낫다.

③ 새로 이사 가는 동네는 그 전 동네보다 못하다.

④ 새로 오는 선생은 Mr. Lewis보다 뛰어날 것이다.

⑤ 왔다 간 다섯 명의 선생 중 Mr. Lewis가 가장 형편없다.

서술형

2 밑줄 친 ⓐ even과 바꿔 쓸 수 없는 말을 찾아 쓰시오.

> much, still, a lot, very, far

Grammar Points! 동사 강조

동사 강조는 do[does, did]로 한다. 동사가 과거일 경우 『did + 현재동사』를 쓴다.

I love you. → I **do** love you. 난 널 정말 사랑한다.

He had a lot of students who **did come** to his classes every week.

그는 매주 그의 수업에 찾아오는 많은 학생들이 있었다.

---

move 이사 가다   regularly 규칙적으로   leave 떠나다   take one's place 자리를 대신하다

A study by the University of Michigan monitored people's moods after two weeks of using SNS(social-networking sites). Their moment-to-moment moods continued getting darker the longer they scrolled through the endless pages of boring statuses and pictures. Users with different network sizes and varying degrees of supportive friends participated, but (A) the result always ended up the same. *The more the participants pressed the "like" button, the worse their moods became. Browsing others' Facebook pages left people with diminished self-images and envious feelings towards their more fortunate acquaintances. For those with self-esteem issues, changing their profile didn't seem to help their self-worth — (B) even if they told lies in a few areas to seem cool.

1 밑줄 친 (A) 부분이 의미하는 바를 가장 잘 나타낸 것은?

① 친구가 많은 이용자일수록 우울감이 더 컸다.

② 이용자의 개인차에도 불구하고 하루 SNS 접속 시간은 비슷했다.

③ 페이스북의 "좋아요" 버튼을 누르는 횟수는 사람마다 달랐다.

④ SNS를 통해 친구를 사귐으로써 우울증을 극복했다.

⑤ SNS 접속 시간이 길수록 이용자들의 기분은 더 우울해졌다.

〔서술형〕

2 밑줄 친 (B) 부분을 우리말로 옮기시오.

_____

Grammar Points! the 비교급, the 비교급: ~하면 할수록 ...하다

한쪽의 정도가 변함에 따라 다른 쪽도 변하는 것을 나타내는 비례 비교 구문이다.
The more you press the "like" button, **the worse** your mood gets.
"좋아요" 버튼을 더 많이 누르면 누를수록 당신의 기분은 더 나빠진다.

monitor 추적 관찰하다. 감시하다   **scroll** 스크롤하다(컴퓨터 화면의 텍스트를 두루마리 읽듯이 상하로 움직이다)   **status** 상태; 지위   **varying** 다양한; 변하는
degree 정도, (각도의 단위인) 도   **supportive** 지지가 되는, 협력적인   **participate** 참가하다   **press** 누르다   **diminish** 줄이다. 떨어뜨리게 하다
(= decline, shrink)   **envious** 시기하는(v. envy 시기하다)   **fortunate** 운 좋은   **acquaintance** 아는 사이   **self-esteem** 자기 존중

During a research experiment a marine biologist placed a shark into a large holding tank and then released several small bait fish into the tank. As you would expect, the shark quickly attacked and ate the smaller fish. The marine biologist then inserted a strong piece of clear fiberglass into the tank, creating two separate partitions. She then put the shark on one side of the fiberglass and a new set of bait fish on the other. Again, the shark quickly attacked. This time, however, the shark slammed into the fiberglass divider and bounced off. Undeterred, the shark kept repeating this behavior every few minutes to no avail. Eventually, about an hour into the experiment, the shark gave up. This experiment was repeated several dozen times over the next few weeks. Each time, the shark got ____(A)____ aggressive and made ____(B)____ attempts to attack the bait fish, until eventually the shark stopped attacking altogether. *The marine biologist then removed the fiberglass divider to see if the shark would attack or not. Surprisingly, the shark had been trained to believe a barrier existed between it and the bait fish, so the bait fish were able to swim wherever they wished, free from harm. Like the shark in this story, we continue to see mental barriers, even when no "real" barrier exists between where we are and where we want to go.

* to no avail 무익하게, 보람도 없이

1 빈칸 (A), (B)에 들어갈 말로 알맞게 짝지어진 것은?

① more – more   ② more – fewer   ③ less – more

④ less – fewer   ⑤ more – no

2 윗글에 나오는 실험 내용과 일치하지 <u>않는</u> 것은?

① 상어는 처음에 유리벽에 반복적으로 부딪치며 먹이를 공격하려 했다.

② 실험 한 시간쯤 후 상어는 공격을 포기했다.

③ 첫 실험 직후부터 상어는 줄곧 물고기를 전혀 공격하려 하지 않았다.

④ 같은 실험이 몇 주 동안 반복해서 이루어졌다.

⑤ 유리벽이 없어진 후에도 미끼 물고기는 상어로부터 안전했다.

3 밑줄 친 부분이 의미하는 바를 가장 잘 나타낸 것은?

① 우리가 가고 싶어 하는 길을 가로막는 장애물이 있을 때

② 현재 우리가 어디에 살고 있는지, 어디로 가고 싶은지 모를 때

③ 우리가 이루고자 하는 목표를 가로막는 장애물이 실제로 없을 때

④ 개인마다 장애물이라고 생각하는 대상이 다를 때

⑤ 진짜 장애물이 우리가 현재 있는 곳이 아닌 다른 곳에 존재할 때

> 서술형

4 Why didn't the shark attack the bait fish after the fiberglass was removed? (Answer in Korean.)

_____

> **Grammar Points!**   명사절을 이끄는 접속사 if
>
> 동사의 목적어인 명사절을 이끌어 '~인지 아닌지'의 뜻을 나타내며, 자주 or not과 함께 쓰인다.
> **The marine biologist then removed the fiberglass divider to see if the shark would attack or not.**
> 그 다음 해양 생물학자는 상어가 공격하는지 안 하는지 보기 위해 섬유 유리 칸막이를 제거했다.

experiment 실험, 실험하다 **marine** 바다의, 해양의 **biologist** 생물학자 **release** 풀어놓다 **bait** 미끼, 먹이 **attack** 공격하다 **insert** 넣다, 끼우다
fiberglass 섬유 유리 **separate** 분리된 (= divided) **partition** 분할, 구획 **slam** 강타하다, 세게 부딪치다 **bounce off** 튕기다 **undeterred** (실패 등에)
꺾이지 않는 **aggressive** 공격적인 (↔ friendly 우호적인) **attempt** 시도; 시도하다 **altogether** 완전히 **remove** 제거하다 **barrier** 장벽, 장애물

Word Check ✕ ✕ ✕

정답 및 해설 p.17

[1-10] 영어는 우리말로, 우리말은 영어로 나타내시오.

1 marine : _____

2 envious : _____

3 diet : _____

4 medical : _____

5 farm-fresh : _____

6 공격하다 : _____

7 상태, 지위 : _____

8 운 좋은 : _____

9 공격적인 : _____

10 정도, 도 : _____

[11-13] 괄호 안에서 알맞은 말을 고르시오.

11 (Raw / Boiled) fish is sometimes dangerous for health.

12 Most painters (stick / store) to their own style of painting.

13 I am grateful for your (sufferable / supportive) comments.

[14-16] 빈칸에 들어갈 말을 〈보기〉에서 골라 알맞은 형태로 쓰시오.

〈보기〉 break   monitor   insert

14 Some of the players may, on occasion, _____ the rules and be penalized.

15 _____ coins into the slot and press for a ticket.

16 Each student's progress is closely _____.

[17-19] 짝지어진 단어의 관계가 같도록 빈칸에 알맞은 말을 쓰시오.

17 destroy : destruction = _____ : removal

18 reception : receptionist = _____ : experimenter

19 diminish : decline = divided : _____

[20-22] 다음의 뜻에 해당하는 단어를 〈보기〉에서 골라 쓰시오.

〈보기〉 available   eager   acquaintance

20 _____ : someone who you have met and know slightly, but not well

21 _____ : being able to find or obtain something

22 _____ : wanting to do or have something very much

Unit 11

도표 · 실용문

✖ 유형 소개

1. 일상생활에서 접하는 도표나 실용문을 올바르게 보고 필요한 실용 정보를 파악할 수 있는지를 확인하는 문제이다.
2. 다양한 도표의 형태와 특징, 읽는 법 등을 평소 숙지해두는 것이 중요하다.
3. 실용문은 주위에서 흔히 볼 수 있는 시설 안내문이나 가입 안내문, 각종 이용법 등이 주로 출제된다.

✖ 유형 전략

Step 1 먼저 도표의 제목과 형태, X축과 Y축이 나타내는 바를 빠르게 파악한다. 그래프 설명문의 첫 문장에서 힌트를 얻을 수 있다.
- 막대그래프: 개별 항목의 수치를 단순 비교
- 선그래프: 수치의 변화 추이를 잘 보여줌
- 원그래프: 전체 100%에서 각 항목이 차지하는 비중을 보여줌

Step 2 그래프 설명문은 항목 간의 수치 비교가 주를 이루므로 배수 표현, 비교 표현이 많다. 비교 표현의 정확한 이해를 바탕으로, 그래프가 보여주는 수치와 선택지 문장의 내용이 일치하는지 꼼꼼히 대조하면서 확인한다.

Step 3 실용 안내문에서도 먼저 전체 제목과 각 하위 분야의 소제목을 보고 안내문 내용의 방향을 미리 파악한다. 금액, 시간, 할인율 등 숫자 정보가 자주 나오므로 유의한다.

Words & Phrases

adult 성인
advanced 고급의
affect (병이) 침범하다, ～에 영향을 주다
applicant 지원자
approximately 대략
category 범주
consult 상담하다
disappear 사라지다
encounter 마주치다
exceed ～을 초과하다
exhibit 전시하다; 전시
garage 차고, 주차장
increase 증가하다 (↔ decrease 감소하다)
participation 참여

permanent 영속하는, 상설의
product 제품
recognition 인정
relief 경감, 구조
respectively 각각의
sore 아픈
submit 제출하다
swell 붓다
symptom 증상
temporary 일시적인
translation 번역
vary 다양하다, 달라지다
virtual reality 가상현실

Example

다음 도표의 내용과 일치하지 <u>않는</u> 것은?

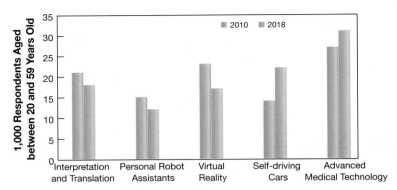

The graph above illustrates the difference of what technology people are looking forward to in the coming industrial revolution, in both 2010 and in 2018. ① The technology people have the highest expectations for is advanced medical technology in both 2010 and 2018, respectively 27% and 31% of respondents. ② Of the five fields, self-driving cars is the least chosen field in 2010, while personal robot assistants is the least in 2018. ③ The percentage change of virtual reality is higher than that of personal robot assistants. ④ Of all categories, the percentage of three fields has fallen but that of two fields has increased. ⑤ The rising rate of self-driving cars is more than twice that of advanced medical technology.

✕ 문제 해결하기

Step 1 **일단 그래프의 제목과 구성 요소 파악하기**
그래프의 제목은 '어떤 기술을 기대하고 있는가?'에 대해 2010년과 2018년을 비교한 표임을 알 수 있다. 대상은 20살에서 59살 사이의 1000명, 단위는 %임을 확인한다. 분야는 5개 분야이며, 분야별로 하락한 것과 증가한 것에 유의한다.

Step 2 **그래프와 대조해가며 설명문 읽기**
increase, decrease, surpass 같은 동사나 the biggest, the least, the highest 등과 (more than) twice -er than, three times as ~ as와 같은 배수사구문도 도표에서는 반드시 익혀야 하는 문법 구문으로 문장 표와 비교해가며 읽는다.

Step 3 **답안 확인하기**
⑤에서 자율자동차의 상승률은 8%, 고급 의료기술은 4% 상승이므로 두 배이지 두 배 이상은 아님을 알 수 있다.

---

look forward to ~을 간절히 바라다 respondent 응답자 interpretation 통역 translation 번역 advanced 고급의 illustrate 설명하다, 예증하다
industrial revolution 산업혁명 respectively 각각의 least 가장 적은 virtual reality 가상현실 increase 증가하다 (↔ decrease 감소하다)

The graph shows the number of refugee applicants and recognized refugees by year in Korea. ① In 2016, a total of 7,542 refugee applications were submitted in Korea. ② In 2015, a total of 105 people received refugee status recognition through the administrative process. ③ The number of refugee applicants has steadily been increasing from 2009 to 2016. ④ 2011 had the lowest rate of refugee recognition ever recorded. ⑤ *The increase in the refugee applicants between 2014 and 2015 is more than twice as high as that in the refugee applicants between 2013 and 2014.

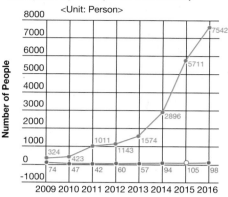

Number of Refugee Applicants and Recognized Refugees, by Year (As of 12/31/2016)

1 도표의 내용과 일치하지 <u>않는</u> 것은?

① ② ③ ④ ⑤

서술형

2 위의 글을 참고하여 다음을 영작하시오.

Tom은 그 멋진 놈보다 두 배나 키가 크다.

_____

Grammar Points!　배수사

'~의 절반'을 나타낼 경우 『half as + 원급 + as ~』로 표현하지만, '~의 두 배'라고 할 때는 『twice as + 원급 + as ~ / twice + 비교급(-er/more-) + than ~』으로 표현한다. 참고로 세 배부터는 three times ~, four times ~를 쓴다.
He is **twice taller than** I. 그는 나보다 2배나 더 크다.
= He is **twice as** tall **as** I.
The TV is used **half as** many hours on the weekends **as** on weekdays.
TV는 주말에 주중 사용 시간의 절반만큼 사용된다.

refugee 난민　applicant 지원자　submit 제출하다　receive 받다　status 지위, 위상　recognition 인정　administrative 행정적인　process 처리과정　steadily 꾸준히　record 기록하다　more than ~ 이상

TopCare Sore Throat Spray Relief

No. 1 pharmacist recommended. Real relief. Real fast. Relieves sore throat pain. Sugar free. Aspirin free. Alcohol 1.87%.

Directions

- Adults and children 6 years of age and older, apply one spray to the affected area.
- Allow medicine to remain in place for at least 15 seconds; then spit out.
- *Use every 2 hours or as directed by a doctor.
- Children under 12 years of age should be supervised in the use of this product.
- Children under 6 years of age, consult a doctor.
- Store at room temperature.

Warning

- Do not use for more than 2 days at a time.
- When using this product, do not exceed the recommended dosage.
- Stop use and ask a doctor if sore mouth symptoms do not improve in 7 days, pain or redness does not disappear, or swelling or fever develops.
- Keep out of reach of children.

1 TopCare Sore Throat Spray Relief에 관한 위 안내문의 내용과 일치하지 <u>않는</u> 것은?

① 목통증 진정제로서 두 시간에 한 번씩 사용하거나 의사의 처방에 따른다.

② 환부에 뿌리고 최소 15초가 지난 후 뱉어낸다.

③ 12세 이하의 어린이가 사용할 시 의사와 상담해야 한다.

④ 한 번에 이틀 이상 사용할 수 없다.

⑤ 약을 사용하여 붓거나 열이 나면 사용을 멈춰야 한다.

서술형

2 밑줄 친 문장을 다음 말로 시작하는 문장으로 바꾸어 쓰시오.

You _____.

Grammar Points!   every + 복수 기간: '매 ~마다'

한정사 every는 '모든'이라는 뜻 외에 시간, 기간 등의 명사와 함께 '매 ~마다'의 단위를 나타낸다.

Use **every 2 hours** or as directed by a doctor. 매 2시간마다 한 번씩 또는 의사의 처방대로 사용하십시오.

sore 아픈   relief 경감, 구조   pharmacist 약사   adult 성인   apply (약을) 바르다, 적용하다   affect (병이) 침범하다, ~에 영향을 주다   in place 제자리에
at least 최소한   spit out 뱉다   supervise 감독하다, 지도하다   product 제품   consult 상담하다   room temperature 상온   at a time 한 번에
exceed ~을 초과하다   dosage 복용량   symptom 증상   redness 적열 상태   disappear 사라지다   swell 붓다   keep out of ~을 멀리 하다

*The graph shows how different age groups of American students spend their money for school in five major spending categories. ① All three age groups of students spend the most on clothing, but elementary and high school students spend far bigger percentages on clothing than college students. ② After clothing, college students spend the most on textbooks, whereas elementary and high school students <u>do so</u> on school supplies. ③ The category that all three age groups spend the least on is software. ④ On textbooks and other expenditures, elementary and high school students spend the same amount of money. ⑤ Elementary and high school students show less dramatic differences than college students do among the five categories of spending habits.

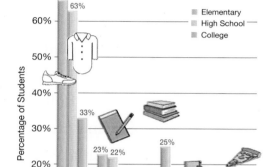

**Money Spent for School
by Type of Students, USA**

SOURCE: Based on data from American Express Retail Index

1 도표의 내용과 일치하지 <u>않는</u> 것은?

①   ②   ③   ④   ⑤

서술형
2 밑줄 친 **do so**가 가리키는 것을 영어로 쓰시오.

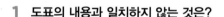

Grammar Points!   간접의문문

의문사가 있는 의문문이 문장의 명사절이 될 때 이를 간접의문문이라고 하며, 『의문사 + 주어 + 동사』의 어순이라는 점에 유의한다.
The graph above shows how <u>different age groups of American students</u> <u>spend</u> their money for
                              S   V   O

school in five major spending categories.

위 그래프는 다섯 가지 주요 지출 항목에 대해 미국의 각 연령별 학생 그룹의 돈의 소비가 어떤지를 보여준다.

---

spend ~ on ... ···에 ~을 지출하다   elementary student 초등학생   whereas ~인 반면에   supply 공급(품), 물자; 공급하다   category 범주
expenditure 지출, 소비 (v. expend 소비하다 / a. expensive 값비싼)

Museum of Science

We promote thoughtful participation in today's increasingly technological society. With over 700 permanent exhibits and ever-changing temporary exhibits, films, and shows, *you can encounter the fresh and unfamiliar.

Ticket Prices

Venues	Adult(12+)		Senior(60+)		Child(3-11)	
	Guest	Member	Guest	Member	Guest	Member
Exhibit Halls	$23.00	FREE	$21.00	FREE	$20.00	FREE
Mugar Omni Theater	$10.00	$10.00	$9.00	$9.00	$8.00	$8.00
Butterfly Garden	$5.00	$3.00	$4.50	$2.50	$4.00	$2.00

Exhibit Halls Hours

Summer Hours: July 5 ~ September 1

• Saturday ~ Thursday, 9:00 a.m. ~ 7:00 p.m.

• Friday, 9:00 a.m. ~ 7:00 p.m.

Regular Hours: September 2 ~ December 31

• Saturday ~ Thursday, 9:00 a.m. ~ 5:00 p.m.

• Friday, 9:00 a.m. ~ 7:00 p.m.

Hours for other venues vary. Find out more at the Museum.

Driving to the Museum?

The Museum's garage provides hourly parking for approximately 850 cars on a first-come, first-served basis. Museum members receive a discount. Parking is available for visitors with disabilities.

1 Museum of Science에 관한 위 안내문의 내용과 일치하지 <u>않는</u> 것은?

① 12세 이상부터 성인 입장료를 내야 한다.
② 일반인과 회원의 입장료가 같은 시설도 있다.
③ 하절기에는 관람 시간이 두 시간 연장된다.
④ 박물관 내 시설들의 개장과 폐장 시간은 각기 다르다.
⑤ 회원을 위한 주차 공간이 따로 마련되어 있다.

2 Museum of Science에 관한 내용과 일치하는 것은?

① 계속 변하는 특설 전시가 700개 이상 된다.
② 회원은 나이에 상관없이 전시관 입장이 무료이다.
③ 나비 정원의 아동 입장은 모두 무료이다.
④ 회원 외에는 주차할 수 없다.
⑤ 장애인 방문객은 주차료가 할인된다.

서술형

3 경로 우대자 회원 두 명이 세 곳을 모두 관람할 경우 입장료는 모두 얼마인지 쓰시오.

_____

Grammar Points! the + 형용사

형용사에 정관사 the를 함께 쓰면 명사 없이 '～한 사람들', 또는 '～한 것'으로 쓰이는 경우가 있다.
You can encounter the fresh and unfamiliar. 당신은 신선하고 낯선 것과 만날 수 있다.

promote 장려하다, 증진하다 (접두사 pro(forward)+mote(move)) **participation** 참여 **permanent** 영속하는, 상설의 **temporary** 일시적인 **exhibit** 전시하다; 전시 **encounter** 마주치다 **venue** 개최지, 장소 **vary** 다양하다, 달라지다 **garage** 차고, 주차장 **approximately** 대략 **first-come, first-served** 선착순의 **disability** 불구, 장애

Word Check ✕ ✕ ✕

정답 및 해설 p.19

[1-10] 영어는 우리말로, 우리말은 영어로 나타내시오.

1 consult : _____
2 swell : _____
3 advanced : _____
4 approximately : _____
5 garage : _____

6 일시의 : _____
7 초과하다 : _____
8 번역 : _____
9 영속하는 : _____
10 전시하다 : _____

[11-13] 괄호 안에서 알맞은 말을 고르시오.

11 How does it (threat / affect) my plans?
12 With everything in (place / location), she started the slide show.
13 Her mood (carries / varies) with the weather.

[14-16] 빈칸에 들어갈 말을 〈보기〉에서 골라 알맞은 형태로 쓰시오.

〈보기〉 submit   relief   supervise

14 He _____ and trained more than 400 volunteers.
15 I wish to _____ a report.
16 The drugs provide _____ from the pain.

17 다음 문장의 밑줄 친 부분과 바꿔 쓸 수 있는 것을 고르시오.

The music <u>affected</u> him deeply.

① included   ② suspected   ③ encountered   ④ influenced

[18-20] 다음의 뜻에 해당하는 단어를 〈보기〉에서 골라 쓰시오.

〈보기〉 expenditure   illustrate   symptom

18 _____ : to make clear or explain by use of examples or comparisons
19 _____ : a change in the condition or appearance of the body that is a sign of disease
20 _____ : the spending or using of resources such as money, time, energy, etc.

Unit 12

주어진 문장의 위치

※ 유형 소개

1. 단락 내의 보충 설명 문장 하나를 빼놓고 이것이 원래 있었던 자리를 찾을 수 있는가를 묻는 문제 유형이다.
2. 단락 안의 문장들은 하나의 주제를 일관되게 설명해야 할 뿐만 아니라 흐름에 있어 논리적인 공백이나 비약이 없어야 한다. 이 유형은 글의 논리적 흐름을 바르게 파악하고 있는지를 평가한다.

※ 유형 전략

Step 1 주어진 문장이 무엇에 관한 내용인지 파악한다. 주어진 문장 속의 접속사, 대명사, 정관사 등에 주목하여 단서로 이용한다.

Step 2 단락 전체를 읽으면서 논리적으로 어색한 부분을 찾는다. 본문에 있는 단서와 주어진 문장에 있는 단서와의 연관성을 확인한다.

Step 3 선택지에 주어진 문장을 넣어 전후 관계가 논리적인지 확인한다.

Words & Phrases

audience 관객, 관중
belong to ~의 것이다, ~에 속하다
challenge 도전하다
civilian 시민, 민간인
community 공동체, 사회
describe 묘사하다, 기술하다
disappear 사라지다
due to ~ 때문에
effort 노력
electricity 전기
enemy 적
expert 전문가
fashionable 유행의, 유행을 따른

frequently 종종, 자주
innocent 죄 없는, 순진무구한
item 품목
means 수단
occur 발생하다, 일어나다
organized 조직화된
preserve 보존하다
responsible 책임이 있는, 원인이 되는
skilled 능숙한, 숙련된
specifically 특히, 명확히
target 표적; 목표로 정하다
temperature 기온
threat 위협 (v. threaten 위협하다)

Example

> Terrorists are not strong enough or organized well enough to target organized armed forces effectively.

Terrorism is the use of violence or the threat of violence against a target audience in order to derive political change. (①) It is, like war, a continuation of politics by other means. (②) Then why do terrorists kill innocent people? (③) So they target a community at its weakest point — its civilians. (④) Terrorists target the least prepared people for an attack. (⑤) In their eyes, civilians are not innocent as they are part of a community that is their enemy. Therefore, in the eyes of the terrorists, they are the enemy.

✕ 문제 해결하기

Step 1 **주어진 문장의 내용 파악하기**
주어진 문장의 내용은 '테러리스트는 군대를 상대할 만큼 강하고 조직화되어 있지 않다'이다.

Step 2 **단락 전체를 읽으면서 논리적으로 어색한 부분 찾기**
처음 두 문장에서 테러리즘이 무엇인가에 관해 설명한 다음 세 번째 문장에서 테러리스트들이 왜 무고한 사람들을 죽이는지 질문을 던지고 있다. 그다음에는 이에 대한 대답이 이어져야 자연스러운데 (③) 뒷부분에는 So로 시작하여 다시 테러리스트가 약한 시민을 공격한다는 내용이 나온다. 따라서 이 자리에 질문에 대한 답, 즉 이유에 해당되는 문장이 나와야 한다.

Step 3 **주어진 문장을 넣고 전후 논리 관계 확인하기**
주어진 문장을 ③에 넣어보면 전후 맥락이 자연스러우므로 정답임을 알 수 있다.

---

target 표적; 목표로 정하다 **organized** 조직화된 **armed forces** 무장 병력 **effectively** 효과적으로 **violence** 폭력 (a. violent 폭력적인) **threat** 위협
(v. threaten 위협하다) **audience** 관객, 관중 **derive** 끌어내다 **political** 정치적인 **continuation** 연속, 지속 **politics** 정치, 정치학 **means** 수단
innocent 죄 없는, 순진무구한 (↔ guilty) **community** 공동체, 사회 **civilian** 시민, 민간인 **attack** 공격 (↔ defense) **enemy** 적

Today, there are more than 7,000 languages spoken on Earth. (①) But by 2100, more than half of those may disappear. (②) In fact, experts say one language dies every two weeks, due to the increasing dominance of larger languages, such as English, Spanish, and Mandarin. (③) *Efforts like National Geographic's Enduring Voices Project are now tracking down and documenting the world's most threatened indigenous languages, such as Tofa, spoken by only thirty people in Siberia, and Magati Ke, from Aboriginal Australia. (④) The hope is to preserve these languages and the cultures they belong to. (⑤)

* Aboriginal 오스트레일리아 원주민의

---

1 글의 흐름으로 보아, 다음 문장이 들어가기에 가장 적절한 곳은?

> So what can be done to keep dialects from disappearing?

①   ②   ③   ④   ⑤

서술형

2 밑줄 친 those가 가리키는 말을 찾아 쓰시오.

_____

Grammar Points!   공통구문

문장 안의 한 요소에 두 개 이상의 어구가 공통으로 연결되는 구문을 공통구문이라고 한다.
Efforts like National Geographic's Enduring Voices Project **are** now **tracking** down and **documenting** the world's most threatened indigenous languages. 내셔널 지오그래픽의 '지속하는 소리 프로젝트'와 같은 노력들이 현재 세계에서 가장 위협받고 있는 토착어들을 추적하여 기록하고 있다. – are에 tracking과 documenting이 공통으로 연결된다.

---

disappear 사라지다   expert 전문가   due to ～ 때문에   dominance 우세, 지배 (a. dominant 지배적인)   effort 노력   track 이동하며 촬영하다, 추적하다   document 기록하다, (상세히) 보도하다   indigenous 토착의, 고유의   preserve 보존하다   belong to ～의 것이다, ～에 속하다   dialect 방언, 파생 언어

In the city of Reykjavik, Iceland, many people get their energy from steam. (①) Power plants drill a hole in the crust to release the hot steam and make a geyser. (②) They use the extremely hot steam to make electricity. (③) *If the steam is not hot enough to make electricity, it's pumped into people's houses to heat them. (④) Around 80 percent of the houses in this very cold city are heated by steam from under the ground, and some of them receive their electricity from the steam, too. (⑤) New Zealand, China, Thailand, and the Philippines all get some of their energy from underground.

* geyser 간헐천

1 글의 흐름으로 보아, 다음 문장이 들어가기에 가장 적절한 곳은?

> More than thirty countries around the world use Earth's power to make energy.

①   ②   ③   ④   ⑤

서술형
2 Reykjavik에서는 땅속에서 나오는 증기를 어떻게 이용하고 있는지 우리말로 쓰시오.

_____

Grammar Points!   enough to부정사

'～할 정도로 충분히 …하다'라는 뜻을 나타낼 때는 enough를 이용하여 『형용사/부사 + enough to부정사』로 표현한다.
If the steam is not **hot enough to make** electricity, it's pumped into people's houses to heat them.
증기가 전기를 만들 정도로 충분히 뜨겁지 않다면 그것은 퍼 올려져 사람들의 집으로 보내 난방을 한다.

steam 증기   power plant 발전소, 동력 장치   crust 지각   release 배출하다 (= give off)   extremely 극단적으로, 몹시   electricity 전기   pump 퍼 올리다   receive 받다

*Who has probably the most dangerous job in the U.S.A.? Perhaps you're thinking a police officer, a miner, a truck driver? Actually, it's a fisherman — specifically a crab fisherman in the Bering Sea. Why is this work so difficult? (①) *A lot of it is done during winter, when temperatures are extremely cold and powerful storms occur frequently. (②) Strong winds can sometimes blow fishermen off their boats into the cold water and are responsible for a number of deaths. (③) In the winter, it is also quite dark, even during the day. (④) Many people die doing this job every year — the most in the U.S.A. (⑤) Why do men and women risk their lives to do this terrifying and difficult work? One reason is money. A skilled fisherman has the potential to earn U.S. $25,000 for working only five weeks at sea.

1 글의 흐름으로 보아, 다음 문장이 들어가기에 가장 적절한 곳은?

> Therefore, fishermen can't rely on their eyes to help them move in the right direction on the boat.

①   ②   ③   ④   ⑤

서술형

2 윗글에 나오는 crab fishermen이라는 직업이 어려운 이유를 우리말로 쓰시오.

_____

Grammar Points!   관계부사의 계속적 용법

관계부사 when과 where는 계속적 용법으로 쓰일 수 있으며 이때 의미는 and then, and there 등과 같다.
A lot of it is done <u>during winter</u>, **when** temperatures are extremely cold and powerful storms occur frequently. 그 일의 많은 부분은 겨울 동안 이루어지는데, 그때는 기온이 몹시 춥고 강력한 폭풍이 자주 일어나는 때이다.

miner 광부   fisherman 어부   specifically 특히, 명확히   crab 게   temperature 기온   storm 폭풍   occur 발생하다, 일어나다   frequently 종종, 자주   responsible 책임이 있는, 원인이 되는   risk one's life 목숨을 걸다   terrifying 두렵게 하는, 무서운   skilled 능숙한, 숙련된   potential 잠재력, 가능성   rely on ~에 의존하다   direction 방향

From the Middle Ages, the rules for clothing in the Western world had been clear: men wore pants and women wore skirts. (①) Amelia Bloomer wanted clothing that allowed women to move more freely. (②) She created "bloomers", a skirt that fell just below the knee with a pair of pants underneath. (③) Most women, however, found bloomers unstylish and they quickly were forgotten. (④) About 50 years later, women working in the coal mines of England challenged the rule again. (⑤) *They came to work wearing pants under their skirts, which they rolled up to their waists to keep them out of the way <u>while on the job</u>. At first people couldn't accept this bold try, but soon more women followed their lead.

When American women went to work in factories during World War I, they also wore trousers. The sight of a woman in pants grew less shocking, but wearing them outside of work was still taboo. Then Hollywood stepped in. Marlene Dietrich, a famous film star, made fashion history when she wore slacks in a 1930 film. Overnight, society had a change of heart about women in pants. Other stars began sporting trousers, fashion magazines described pants a fashionable item, and women listened.

1 글의 흐름으로 보아, 다음 문장이 들어가기에 가장 적절한 곳은?

> But in the early 1850s, one woman decided that she'd had enough of heavy skirts.

①   ②   ③   ④   ⑤

2 윗글의 제목으로 가장 적절한 것은?

① The Origin of Bloomers
② Ancient and Modern Clothing Rules
③ How Pants Became Women's Clothes
④ Who Made Pants Popular Among Men
⑤ Some Interesting Fashion History

3 윗글의 내용과 일치하지 <u>않는</u> 것은?

① 블루머는 등장하자마자 크게 유행했다.
② 20세기 초에 일하는 여성들이 바지를 입기 시작했다.
③ 바지를 입던 초기 시절 여성들은 치마와 함께 입었다.
④ 대개의 여성들은 1920년대까지 직장 밖에서 바지를 입지는 않았다.
⑤ 한 유명 여배우가 초기 바지에 대한 여성들의 태도를 바꾸어 놓았다.

서술형

4 밑줄 친 **while on the job**에서 생략된 말을 쓰시오.

while _____ on the job

Grammar Points!   계속적 용법의 관계대명사

관계대명사 which와 who는 계속적 용법으로 쓰여 선행사를 부연 설명할 수 있다.
They came to work wearing pants under <u>their skirts</u>, **which** they rolled up to their waists to keep them out of the way while on the job. 그들은 치마 안에 바지를 입은 채 출근했는데 일하는 동안에는 치마가 방해되지 않도록 그것을 허리까지 말아 올렸다.

---

underneath ~의 아래에, 밑에   unstylish 유행에 맞지 않는   coal mine 탄광   challenge 도전하다   roll up 말아 올리다   keep ~ out of the way ~을 방해가 되지 않도록 하다   bold 대담한   taboo 금기   step in 개입하다, 간섭하다   slacks 바지   sport 과시하다, 자랑스럽게 입다   describe 묘사하다, 기술하다   fashionable 유행의, 유행을 따른   item 품목

Word Check ✕ ✕ ✕

정답 및 해설 p.20

[1-10] 영어는 우리말로, 우리말은 영어로 나타내시오.

1 threaten : _____

2 audience : _____

3 derive : _____

4 continuation : _____

5 means : _____

6 시민, 민간인 : _____

7 적 : _____

8 방언 : _____

9 잠재력, 가능성 : _____

10 금기 : _____

[11-13] 괄호 안에서 알맞은 말을 고르시오.

11 The company must reduce costs to compete (effectively / extremely).

12 You should put more (effort / expert) into your work.

13 Jake is (described / responsible) for designing the entire project.

[14-16] 빈칸에 들어갈 말을 〈보기〉에서 골라 알맞은 형태로 쓰시오.

〈보기〉 keep   rely   step

14 As babies, we _____ entirely _____ others for food.

15 Add a little more flour to _____ it _____ being too sticky.

16 A local businessman tried to _____ _____ with a large donation for the school.

[17-19] 짝지어진 단어의 관계가 같도록 빈칸에 알맞은 말을 쓰시오.

17 fashionable : unstylish = guilty : _____

18 politics : political = _____ : violent

19 appear : disappear = _____ : defense

[20-22] 다음의 뜻에 해당하는 단어를 〈보기〉에서 골라 쓰시오.

〈보기〉 dominant   indigenous   organized

20 _____ : native, belonging to the country in which something is found

21 _____ : more powerful, successful, or important than other people or things

22 _____ : doing something together in a structured way

Unit 13

무관한 문장

✕ 유형 소개

1. 주어진 글에서 논리적인 흐름과 맞지 않는 한 문장을 고르게 함으로써 글의 논리를 파악할 수 있는지 확인하는 문제 유형이다.
2. 대개 글의 주요 소재를 언급하기는 하지만 주제와는 동떨어져 있어서 주제를 뒷받침하지 못하는 문장이 정답이 된다.
3. 주제 또는 대의를 바르게 파악하면 크게 어렵지 않게 풀 수 있는 유형이다.

✕ 유형 전략

Step 1 첫 부분에 주어지는 문장들을 통해 대강의 주제를 파악한다.

Step 2 읽으면서 글의 전체적인 의미 흐름에 어울리지 않는, 즉 주제를 뒷받침하지 않는 문장이 있으면 체크한다.

Step 3 체크한 문장을 빼고 그 앞뒤 문장을 바로 연결해서 읽었을 때 글의 흐름이 자연스러운지 확인한다.

Words & Phrases

analyze 분석하다 (*n.* analysis 분석)
assignment 과제
as usual 평소대로
at a time 한 번에
average 평균
contaminate 오염시키다
deadline 마감 시간
divide 나누다
employee 고용인 (*cf.* employer 고용주)
empty 비우다; 텅 빈
endure 참다, 견디다
essential 필수의, 본질적인
extra 추가적인
germ 세균, 병균

motivate 동기를 주다
oral 구두의, 구술의
particle 극히 작은 조각, 분자
present 제출하다; 출석한
presentation 발표, 제출
put off 미루다, 연기하다
region 지역
resource 자원
reward 보수; 보수를 주다
square 정사각형, 평방
surface 표면
survive 생존하다, 살아남다
task 임무, 과업
valuable 귀중한, 소중한

Example

다음 글에서 전체 흐름과 관계 <u>없는</u> 문장은?

정답 및 해설 p.21

Many kids help out around the house with chores such as emptying the dishwasher and taking out the trash. In exchange, some kids get allowances or other rewards such as extra computer time. ① But some people do not think that kids should get rewards for doing chores. ② They believe that by rewarding kids, parents are sending a message that work isn't worth doing unless you get something in return. ③ Children who do household chores a lot are likely to grow up to be a responsible adult. ④ Other people believe that getting a cash allowance or other reward motivates kids to do chores. ⑤ They think it can also teach them real world lessons about how people need to work to earn money.

✕ 문제 해결하기

Step 1 **주어진 문장으로 주제 파악하기**
서두에 주어진 문장에서 어린이들이 집안일을 하고 보상을 받는다고 언급하고 있으므로 어린이들이 집안일을 하고 보상을 받는 점이 주제이며 후속 문장들에서 이 문제를 언급할 것임을 알 수 있다.

Step 2 **주제를 뒷받침하지 않는 문장 찾기**
③은 집안일을 하는 어린이의 성장 후 특징을 언급하고 있으므로 어린이의 집안일 하기와 보상이라는 주제와는 무관하다.

Step 3 **선택한 문장을 빼고 앞뒤 문장을 연결하여 읽기**
③번 문장을 빼더라도 ②번 문장까지 보상 반대론자의 주장이 나온 다음 ④번부터는 보상 찬성자들의 주장이 자연스럽게 연결됨을 알 수 있다.

Step 4 **답안 확인하기**
따라서 ③번 문장은 글의 주제를 뒷받침하지 못하는 데다 빼고 읽어도 남은 문장들이 자연스럽게 연결되므로 ③이 정답임을 알 수 있다.

chore 허드렛일, 집안일   empty 비우다; 텅 빈   dishwasher 식기 세척기   in exchange 교환하여, 그 대신   allowance 용돈, 수당   reward 보수; 보수를 주다   extra 추가적인   be worth -ing ～할 가치가 있다   in return 보답으로, 그 대신에   motivate 동기를 주다   lesson 교훈

Residents of the Eastern, Midwestern and even Southern regions of the United States are really feeling the wrath of winter this year, and are probably thinking that *nobody in the world has <u>it</u> as bad as they do. However, they are wrong. ① The people of Yakutsk in Russia have been enduring even worse weather for centuries, and have actually grown to like it. ② Winter weather can cause a number of problems ranging from water leaks to burst pipes. ③ The world's coldest city endures through winter temperatures that average -45°C. ④ Kids only get days off from school when temperatures get below -55°C. ⑤ For the adults, they almost always work as usual, which often means spending hours selling wares in outdoor markets.

1 윗글에서 전체 흐름과 관계 <u>없는</u> 문장은?

①　　　　　②　　　　　③　　　　　④　　　　　⑤

서술형

2 밑줄 친 <u>it</u>이 가리키는 것을 찾아 쓰시오.

_____

Grammar Points!　원급의 최상급 의미

『no ~ as … as A』의 형태로 '아무것도 A만큼 …하지 않다, A가 가장 …하다'라는 의미의 최상급을 나타낸다.
Nobody in the world has it **as** bad **as** they do. 세상의 그 누구도 그들만큼 심하게 그것(겨울의 혹독함)을 겪고 있지는 않다.

resident 거주자 (v. reside 거주하다)　Midwestern 중서부의　region 지역　wrath 독독함, 분노　bad 심하게　range 줄짓다, 뻗어있다　leak 누수, 샘, 새다　burst 파열시키다　endure 참다, 견디다　average 평균　get a day off 하루 쉬다　as usual 평소대로　ware 상품

Some places you encounter in your daily life are seriously contaminated with germs. For example, office desks have hundreds of times more bacteria per square inch <u>than do the toilet seats in those same buildings.</u> ① Also you should avoid eating in front of your computer because food particles contribute to germs. ② Rubbing your hands under a dryer can boost the number of bacteria on your skin by up to 45 percent. ③ Not all bacteria are harmful, and some bacteria that live in your body are actually good for you. ④ Did you know that sinks are the most germ-ridden surface in public restrooms? ⑤ *The dampness helps microorganisms survive.

1 윗글에서 전체 흐름과 관계 <u>없는</u> 문장은?

①   ②   ③   ④   ⑤

서술형
2 밑줄 친 부분을 우리말로 옮기시오.

_____

Grammar Points!   준사역동사 help

'(목적어)가 ~하는 것을 돕다'라는 뜻으로 help가 쓰일 때 목적격 보어로 to부정사나 원형부정사를 모두 사용할 수 있다.
The dampness helps microorganisms (to) survive. 습기는 미생물이 생존하는 것을 돕는다.

---

contaminate 오염시키다   germ 세균, 병균   square 정사각형, 평방   avoid 피하다, 방지하다   particle 극히 작은 조각, 분자   contribute to ~에 기여하다   rub 문지르다   boost 증대시키다   up to ~까지   harmful 해로운   ridden (보통 합성어에서) ~이 들끓는, ~에 지배당하는   surface 표면 dampness 습기 (a. damp 축축한)   microorganism 미생물   survive 생존하다, 살아남다

Have you heard about the government shutdown in the US? Here's how it happens. The federal government in Washington makes decisions on how to spend the country's money and presents a budget each year. ① *A government is the system by which a state is governed and affects every human activity in many important ways. ② In order to pass the budget, Congress needs to agree, but in general, Democrats and Republicans have very different ideas on how to best use that money. ③ If <u>they</u> don't agree until their deadline, the government partially shuts down. ④ "Essential" federal government employees like soldiers, mailmen, etc., all still have their jobs. ⑤ But the national parks and zoos are closed and the workers lose their jobs and don't get paid.

* Democrat (미국) 민주당원   * Republican (미국) 공화당원

1 윗글에서 전체 흐름과 관계 없는 문장은?

①   ②   ③   ④   ⑤

서술형

2 밑줄 친 **they**가 가리키는 것을 윗글에서 찾아 쓰시오.

_____

Grammar Points!   관계대명사와 전치사

관계대명사가 전치사의 목적어인 경우 관계대명사 앞에 전치사가 온다.
A government is <u>the system</u> **by which** a state is governed. 정부란 국가가 통치되는 시스템이다.
← A government is <u>the system</u>. + A state is governed **by the system.**

shutdown 일시 휴업, 폐쇄 (*cf.* shut down 폐쇄하다, 휴업하다) federal 연방의, 연맹의 make a decision on ~에 대해 결정하다 present 제출하다; 출석한 budget 예산안 affect ~에 영향을 주다 Congress 의회, 국회 deadline 마감 시간 partially 부분적으로 essential 필수의, 본질적인 employee 고용인 (*cf.* employer 고용주)

*Do you always put off doing things you don't like until the last minute? The curse of procrastination can keep you from reaching goals such as getting a promotion or raising your grade-point average. To stop procrastinating, start off by analyzing why you don't like to do the task. _____(A)_____ you might not like preparing for an oral presentation because almost everyone who has to talk in front of people gets nervous. ① Then, divide the task up into small pieces; if you have to read twenty pages, just read five pages at a time. ② This is called "chunking," and it makes the assignment ⓐ (seem) less intimidating. ③ Even though time is one of the most valuable resources we have, people seem content to just watch time ⓑ (pass) by in front of them. ④ When you finish, reward yourself with something you like, such as calling a friend or buying a new CD. ⑤ Your greatest reward, _____(B)_____, will be high grades or a successful presentation.

1 윗글에서 전체 흐름과 관계 <u>없는</u> 문장은?

①   ②   ③   ④   ⑤

2 빈칸 (A), (B)에 들어갈 말로 가장 적절한 것은?

	(A)		(B)
①	In contrast	……	as a result
②	Otherwise	……	in contrast
③	In contrast	……	otherwise
④	For example	……	in addition
⑤	For example	……	however

3 procrastination에 관한 윗글의 내용과 일치하지 <u>않는</u> 것은?

① 목표를 성취하는 것을 방해한다.
② 예방하려면 주어진 일이 싫은 이유부터 알아낸다.
③ 마음이 불안한 사람이 주로 겪는 문제이다.
④ 주어진 일을 작게 나눠 함으로써도 예방할 수 있다.
⑤ 일이 끝났을 때 주어지는 보상이 있으면 피할 수 있다.

> 서술형

4 ⓐ와 ⓑ 각각 괄호 안의 말을 알맞은 형태로 쓰시오.

ⓐ _____   ⓑ _____

Grammar Points!   시간을 나타내는 전치사

시간을 나타내는 전치사 until, till, before, after, since 등은 부사절의 접속사로도 쓰인다.
Do you always put off doing things you don't like until the last minute?
당신은 하기 싫어하는 일을 하는 것을 마지막 순간까지 항상 미루는가?
Let's wait until the rain stops. 비가 그칠 때까지 기다리자.

---

put off 미루다, 연기하다   curse 저주, 불행; 저주하다   procrastination 지연 (v. procrastinate 지연하다)   promotion 승진   grade-point average 성적 평가점 평균   analyze 분석하다 (n. analysis 분석)   task 임무, 과업   prepare for ~에 대해 준비하다   oral 구두의, 구술의   presentation 발표, 제출   divide 나누다   at a time 한 번에   assignment 과제   intimidate 위협하다   valuable 귀중한, 소중한   resource 자원   content 만족하는; 내용

Word Check ✕ ✕ ✕

정답 및 해설 p.22

[1-10] 영어는 우리말로, 우리말은 영어로 나타내시오.

1   survive : _____
2   particle : _____
3   employee : _____
4   divide : _____
5   content : _____

6   동기를 주다 : _____
7   예산안 : _____
8   분석하다 : _____
9   지연 : _____
10 연방의, 연맹의 : _____

[11-13] 괄호 안에서 알맞은 말을 고르시오.

11 We have (gotten / put) off our camping trip until next month.
12 We'll send them cake and they'll send us cookies in (return / charge).
13 She wiped the table with a (moisture / damp) cloth.

[14-16] 빈칸에 들어갈 말을 〈보기〉에서 골라 알맞은 형태로 쓰시오.

〈보기〉 worth   contaminate   empty

14 The idea is not _____ discussing. Let's forget about it.
15 The house was bare and _____.
16 The river has been _____ with toxic wastes.

[17-18] 짝지어진 단어의 관계가 같도록 빈칸에 알맞은 말을 쓰시오.

17 gift : present = _____ : precious
18 survive : survivor = reside : _____

[19-21] 다음의 뜻에 해당하는 단어를 〈보기〉에서 골라 쓰시오.

〈보기〉 endure   intimidate   chore

19 _____ : to make frightened
20 _____ : to undergo hardship, to remain firm
21 _____ : a small routine task, especially a domestic one

Unit
14

이어질 글의
순서 추론

Words & Phrases

adverse 반대의, 해로운
annually 매년, 해마다
bean 콩
concept 개념
creation 창조
deal with 다루다, 대처하다
disability 무능, 불구
effectiveness 유효성, 효과적임
ensure ～을 책임지다, 보증하다
exist 존재하다
generation 세대
hero 영웅

infection 감염
infant 유아
legend 전설
myth 신화
numerous 무수히 많은
obtain 얻다, 획득하다
permanent 영구적인 (↔ temporary 일시적인)
provide 제공하다
public place 공공장소
regulate 규제하다, 관리하다
remain ～인 채로 남아있다
work 작품

Example

주어진 글에 이어질 순서로 가장 적절한 것은?

정답 및 해설 p.22

All cultures around the world have unique legends and traditions that have been passed down over generations. Many myths refer to gods or supernatural heroes who are responsible for occurrences in the world.

(A) From this tiny piece of earth, the entire world takes shape.

(B) And many creation myths, especially from some of North America's native cultures, tell of an earth-diver represented as an animal that brings a piece of sand or mud up from the deep sea.

(C) For example, Norse mythology tells of the red-bearded Thor, the god of thunder, who is responsible for creating lightning and thunderstorms.

① (A) − (B) − (C)　　② (B) − (C) − (A)　　③ (B) − (A) − (C)
④ (C) − (A) − (B)　　⑤ (C) − (B) − (A)

✕ 문제 해결하기

Step 1 **주어진 문장을 통해 주제 파악하기**
주어진 부분의 두 번째 문장이 이 글의 주제문이며 세상에서 일어나는 사건들의 원인으로 생각되는 신화 속 신들과 영웅들이 이 글의 주제이다. 따라서 여러 신화에 등장하는 신들과 영웅에 대한 예시가 이어질 것임을 예측할 수 있다.

Step 2 **연결어와 지시어, 대명사에 주목하여 전후 관계 파악하기**
(C)의 For example이 예시를 나타내는 연결어이므로 주어진 문장 바로 뒤에 올 것임을 알 수 있다. (B)의 And는 또 다른 예시를 첨가하는 것이므로 (C) 다음에 올 수 있다. (A)의 this는 앞에 나온 작은 조각의 흙을 가리키므로 이에 대한 언급이 있는 (B) 다음에 온다는 것을 알 수 있다.

Step 3 **배열한 순서가 자연스러운지 확인하기**
주어진 부분에 이어 (C)–(B)–(A) 순서로 재배열하여 글을 읽어보면 연결이 자연스러움을 확인할 수 있다.

---

unique 독특한　legend 전설　pass down (대대로) 전하다　generation 세대　myth 신화　supernatural 초자연적인　hero 영웅　occurrence 사건, 생긴 일　entire 전체의　take shape 형태를 이루다　creation 창조　represent 대표하다, 나타내다　Norse mythology 북유럽 신화　red-bearded 붉은 수염의　lightning 번개　thunderstorm (뇌우를 동반한) 폭풍우

Over a century after his death, van Gogh still remains extremely popular. His story gives people something they need. *We find pieces of ourselves in him.

(A) But they are also buying a piece of his story, which, like his work, will live on forever.

(B) This may also explain the high prices paid for van Gogh's work. His *Portrait of Dr. Gachet* sold in 1990 for more than $80 million to a Japanese businessman, breaking the world record for an art purchase.

(C) Many of his other works have also sold for millions. Of course, people are buying great art when they purchase one of van Gogh's paintings.

1 주어진 글에 이어질 순서로 가장 적절한 것은?

① (A) − (C) − (B)　② (B) − (A) − (C)　③ (B) − (C) − (A)
④ (C) − (A) − (B)　⑤ (C) − (B) − (A)

서술형
2 밑줄 친 This가 가리키는 내용을 우리말로 쓰시오.

_____

Grammar Points!　재귀대명사

목적어가 주어와 같을 때 재귀대명사를 쓴다(재귀적 용법). 이밖에도 주어, 목적어, 보어를 강조하는 강조 용법으로도 재귀대명사를 쓸 수 있다.

We find pieces of ourselves in him. 우리는 그에게서 우리 자신의 일부분을 발견한다. – 재귀적 용법
Life itself is an unsolved mystery. 인생은 그 자체가 풀리지 않는 신비이다. – 강조 용법

remain ~인 채로 남아있다　popular 인기 있는　work 작품　live on 계속해 살다. (명성 따위가) 남다　portrait 초상화　break the record 기록을 깨다
purchase 구매; 구매하다

> Our early ancestors were hunter-gatherers who obtained food by hunting and searching for edible wild plants. They needed strong bones, which included large, strong jaws that enabled them to eat tough, uncooked foods.

(A) Consequently, the human skeleton underwent radical changes. Over time, the human jaw became smaller and changed shape.

(B) As a result of both dietary changes and a less active lifestyle other bones also evolved, and in particular joints became lighter.

(C) When our ancestors developed agriculture, however, their diet changed. They began growing plants such as grains and beans, and raising animals for food; *they also started cooking their foods, making them softer and easier to chew.

1 주어진 글에 이어질 순서로 가장 적절한 것은?

① (A) − (C) − (B) ② (B) − (A) − (C) ③ (B) − (C) − (A)
④ (C) − (A) − (B) ⑤ (C) − (B) − (A)

서술형

2 옛날 선조들의 골격과 뼈가 변하게 된 결정적인 계기가 된 사건을 우리말로 쓰시오.

Grammar Points! 분사구문 해석 요령

앞에 문장이 나오고 콤마(,) 뒤에 분사구문이 나오면 **앞에서부터 해석**하며, 뒤에 오는 분사구문의 경우 '접속사(and, but, for, though) + 동사(*주절의 시제와 일치)'로 해석한다.

They also started cooking their foods, **making** them softer and easier to chew.
= They also started cooking their foods **and made** them softer and easier to chew.
그들은 또한 음식을 요리하기 시작했다. 그래서 그 음식을 연하게 하여 씹기 쉽게 했다.

---

ancestor 조상, 선조 hunter-gatherer 수렵채집인 obtain 얻다, 획득하다 search for ~을 찾다 edible 먹을 수 있는 wild plant 야생 식물 jaw 턱
as a result of ~의 결과로 dietary 식이요법의 active 활동적인 lifestyle 양식 evolve 진화하다 agriculture 농업 grain 곡물 bean 콩 raise
animals 동물을 기르다 easier to chew 씹기 쉬운

The concept of self-service is (part, a, much, so) of American culture that it expresses itself in the small details of life. If you visit friends and plan to stay for a while, they may not serve you or cater to your every need.

(A) Rather, *it is a simple invitation for you to make yourself at home and feel free to do things without asking.

(B) Instead, they might extend their hospitality by saying, "Help yourself!" This does not mean that you are unwelcome or that they refuse to be a good host.

(C) This call to "help yourself" can be found at lots of stores and public places. For example, many gas stations provide a self-service island where one can pump one's own gas.

1 주어진 글에 이어질 순서로 가장 적절한 것은?

① (A) − (C) − (B)   ② (B) − (A) − (C)   ③ (B) − (C) − (A)
④ (C) − (A) − (B)   ⑤ (C) − (B) − (A)

서술형
2 괄호 안에 주어진 단어들을 어법에 맞게 재배열하시오.

_____

Grammar Points!   보어로 쓰이는 전치사구

전치사구는 형용사 역할을 할 수 있으므로 문장에서 주격 보어나 목적격 보어로 쓰일 수 있다.
It is a simple invitation for you to make yourself at home and feel free to do things without asking.
그것은 당신이 집에서처럼 편히 지내며 묻지 않고 자유롭게 일들을 하라는 단순한 권유이다.

concept 개념 express 표현하다 cater 요구에 응하다 invitation 권유; 초대 make oneself at home (자기 집에 있는 것처럼) 편히 하다 feel free to-v 자유롭게 ~하다 extend 베풀다, 연장하다 hospitality 환대, 후한 대접 refuse 거부하다 (*n.* refusal 거부) public place 공공장소 provide 제공하다

(A)

The US Food and Drug Administration (FDA) regulates all vaccines to ensure safety and effectiveness. No federal laws mandating vaccination exist, but all fifty states require certain vaccinations (exemptions allowed) for children entering public schools.

(B)

Lots of experts, however, contend that children's immune systems can deal with those infections naturally, and that the possible side effects of vaccination, including seizures, paralysis, and death, are not worth the risk of safeguarding against non-life threatening illnesses. Numerous studies have suggested that vaccines may trigger problems like autism and ADHD.

(C)

*It can't be denied that vaccination was one of the greatest health developments of the 20th century. Serious illnesses, including rubella, diphtheria, and whooping cough, which once killed thousands of infants annually are now prevented by vaccination.

(D)

Nevertheless, about 30,000 cases of adverse reactions to vaccines have been reported annually to the federal government since 1990, with 13% classified as serious, meaning associated with permanent disability, life-threatening illness, or death.

* autism 자폐증   * rubella 풍진   * whopping cough 백일해

1 주어진 글 (A)에 이어질 순서로 가장 적절한 것은?

① (B) − (D) − (C) ② (C) − (B) − (D) ③ (C) − (D) − (B)
④ (D) − (B) − (C) ⑤ (D) − (C) − (B)

2 윗글의 주제로 가장 적절한 것은?

① The history of vaccination in the U.S.
② Benefits and dangers of vaccination
③ The necessity of vaccination for children
④ The kinds of diseases caused by vaccines
⑤ Reasons for ceasing vaccination for children

3 윗글의 내용과 일치하지 <u>않는</u> 것은?

① 백신은 미 식약청에서 안전성을 보증하고 있다.
② 취학 아동은 연방법에 의해 예방접종을 의무적으로 해야 한다.
③ 연간 4000건 가까이 심각한 백신 부작용이 보고되고 있다.
④ 백신이 자폐증을 유발할 수 있다는 연구가 있다.
⑤ 백신은 유아 사망률을 낮춘 20세기 최대의 의학적 진보 중 하나이다.

서술형

4 윗글에서 많은 전문가들이 백신에 반대하는 이유를 찾아 우리말로 쓰시오.

_____

Grammar Points! 가주어 it, 진주어 that절 구문

접속사 that이 이끄는 절이 문장의 주어일 때 가주어 it을 주어 자리에 두고 that절은 문장 뒤에 놓는다.
It can't be denied **that** vaccination was one of the greatest health developments of the 20th century. 예방접종이 20세기 가장 위대한 건강상의 발전 중 하나라는 것은 부인할 수 없다.

---

regulate 규제하다, 관리하다   **ensure** ∼을 책임지다, 보증하다   **effectiveness** 유효성, 효과적임   **mandate** 위임하다, 명령하다   **exist** 존재하다   **exemption** (의무 등의) 면제   **contend** 주장하다   **deal with** 다루다, 대처하다   **infection** 감염   **side effect** 부작용   **seizure** 발작   **paralysis** 마비   **worth the risk** 위험을 감수할 가치가 있는   **numerous** 무수히 많은   **trigger** 유발하다   **annually** 매년, 해마다   **adverse** 반대의, 해로운   **permanent** 영구적인 (↔ temporary 일시적인)   **disability** 무능, 불구

Word Check ✕ ✕ ✕

정답 및 해설 p.23

[1-10] 영어는 우리말로, 우리말은 영어로 나타내시오.

1   unique : _____

2   seizure : _____

3   exemption : _____

4   vaccination : _____

5   safeguard : _____

6   세대 : _____

7   콩 : _____

8   개념 : _____

9   유발하다 : _____

10   무능, 불구 : _____

[11-13] 괄호 안에서 알맞은 말을 고르시오.

11   It is the company's responsibility to (ensure / trigger) the safety of its workers.

12   Hormones (contend / regulate) some bodily functions and control growth.

13   Thank you very much for your (hospitalization / hospitality) during my stay here.

[14-16] 빈칸에 들어갈 말을 〈보기〉에서 골라 알맞은 형태로 쓰시오.

〈보기〉 refuse   obtain   expressed

14   The information may be difficult to _____ .

15   We _____ our thought on the subject.

16   He _____ the job.

[17-19] 짝지어진 단어의 관계가 같도록 빈칸에 알맞은 말을 쓰시오.

17   create : creation = refuse : _____

18   argue : argument = invite : _____

19   physical : mental = temporary : _____

[20-22] 다음의 뜻에 해당하는 단어를 〈보기〉에서 골라 쓰시오.

〈보기〉 legend   generation   mandate

20   _____ : direct or require to do something

21   _____ : a story from the past that is believed by many people but cannot be proved to be true

22   _____ : a group of people born and living during the same time

Unit
15

어휘 추론

✕ 유형 소개

1. 문맥에 맞거나 문맥상 적절하지 않은 낱말을 고르는 문제 유형으로 출제된다.
2. 어려운 낱말의 뜻을 아는지 보다는 문맥을 이해하고 문맥에 맞는 낱말을 파악할 수 있는지를 확인하는 문제이다.
3. 오답 선택지는 문맥에 반대되는 단어인 경우가 많으므로 결국 문맥을 잘 이해하는 것이 이 유형 문제를 해결하는 관건이다.

✕ 유형 전략

Step 1 문맥을 바르게 파악하는 것이 중요하므로 서두에 주어지는 문장들을 통해 먼저 대강의 주제를 파악한다.

Step 2 글의 주제와 주위 문맥을 바탕으로, 선택지가 있는 문장이 전체적으로 어떤 의미가 되어야 하는지 판단한다.

Step 3 주어진 단어들 중 가장 적절한 낱말을 고른다.

Words & Phrases

attention 집중, 주의
achieve 달성하다
annoy 괴롭히다
barrier 장애물, 울타리
cause 원인 (↔ effect 결과)
chest 가슴
committee 위원회
device 장치, 고안물
debut 첫 무대, 데뷔
draw (액체 등을) 퍼 올리다
decrease 감소하다 (↔ increase 증가하다)
event 사건, 종목
fit ~을 설비하다, 달다

fix 고정시키다, 수리하다
imagine 상상하다
misty 안개 낀, 희미한
mystery 신비
nervousness 불안
perform 공연하다, 수행하다
place 두다, 놓다; 장소
pressure 압력
remove 제거하다
spin 회전
terrified 무서워하는, 겁이 난
vibrate 진동하다
worthy 가치 있는

Example

(A), (B), (C)의 각 네모 안에서 문맥에 맞는 낱말로 가장 적절한 것은?

Someone was drawing water and my teacher placed my hand under the spout. As the cool stream flowed out suddenly over one hand she spelled into the other the word *water* – first slowly, then rapidly. I stood still, my whole attention (A) fixed / acted upon the motions of her fingers. Suddenly I felt a misty consciousness as of something forgotten. And somehow the mystery of language was (B) covered / revealed to me. I knew then that "w-a-t-e-r" meant the wonderful cool something that was flowing over my hand. The living word awakened my soul, gave it light, hope, joy, set it free. There were (C) paths / barriers still, but they could in time be swept away.

	(A)		(B)		(C)
①	acted	·····	revealed	·····	barriers
②	acted	·····	covered	·····	barriers
③	fixed	·····	covered	·····	paths
④	fixed	·····	revealed	·····	barriers
⑤	acted	·····	revealed	·····	paths

✕ 문제 해결하기

Step 1 글의 주제 파악하기
서두 부분에서 필자의 선생님이 필자에게 water란 말을 가르쳐주는 장면이 나오는 것으로 보아 이와 관련된 경험이나 느낌이 주제일 것임을 알 수 있다.

Step 2 선택지 문장의 적절한 의미 판단하기
(A) I stood still, my whole attention이란 말로 보아 필자가 '온 집중력을 고정시켰다'가 적절하다. (B) 앞뒤 문맥상 water의 의미를 발견하게 되는 과정이 나오므로 '언어의 신비가 드러났다'가 적절하다. (C) 없어지는 걸 긍정적으로 보는 것으로 보아 부정적인 낱말이 적절하다.

Step 3 적절한 낱말 고르기
선택지 문장의 적절한 의미를 추론해 봤을 때 (A)는 fixed, (B)는 revealed, (C)는 barriers가 올바른 낱말임을 알 수 있다.

draw (액체 등을) 퍼 올리다　place 두다, 놓다; 장소　spout (주전자 등의) 주둥이, 물꼭지　flow out 흘러나오다　spell 철자를 쓰다[말하다]　attention 집중, 주의　fix 고정시키다, 수리하다　misty 안개 낀, 희미한　consciousness 의식, 자각 (*a.* conscious 의식하는, 알고 있는)　mystery 신비　reveal 드러내다, 폭로하다　set free 해방하다　path 길　barrier 장애물, 울타리　sweep away 일소하다, 완전히 없애다

*You must have all imagined how terrified Peeta and Katniss were in the sci-fi novel *The Hunger Games*. However, you probably did not feel like you were in their shoes. That is what researchers at MIT are trying to (A) ⌈avoid / achieve⌉ with a new device that they call Sensory Fiction. The product is comprised of two components. One is the book that is fitted with special sensors. The other is a vest that is connected to the book and then worn by the reader. During a suspenseful passage, the vest may vibrate and help (B) ⌈increase / decrease⌉ the reader's heart rate to mimic excitement or nervousness. Real (C) ⌈happiness / fear⌉ can be felt thanks to the compression of the reader's chest by the pressure bags inside the vest.

1 (A), (B), (C)의 각 네모 안에서 문맥에 맞는 낱말로 가장 적절한 것은?

	(A)		(B)		(C)
①	avoid	······	increase	······	fear
②	achieve	······	increase	······	fear
③	avoid	······	decrease	······	happiness
④	achieve	······	decrease	······	happiness
⑤	avoid	······	increase	······	happiness

[서술형]

2 다음 괄호 안의 말을 바르게 배열하여 우리말과 뜻이 같게 하시오.

저것은 우리가 해야 하는 것이다.

That is _____. (we, do, should, what)

Grammar Points! 과거 사실에 대한 강한 추측

과거 사실에 대하여 '~했음에 틀림없다'라는 의미는 『must + have p.p.』의 형태로 나타낸다.
You **must have** all **imagined** how terrified Peeta and Katniss were in the sci-fi novel *The Hunger Games*. 공상과학 소설인 "헝거 게임"에서 Peeta와 Katniss가 얼마나 무서웠을지 여러분 모두가 상상했음에 틀림없다.

imagine 상상하다   terrified 무서워하는, 겁이 난   be in one's shoes 그 사람의 입장이 되다   achieve 달성하다   device 장치, 고안물   sensory 감각의 (*n.* sensor 감지장치)   be comprised of ~로 구성되다   fit ~을 설비하다, 달다   vest 조끼   connect 연결시키다   suspenseful 애태우게 하는, 긴장하게 하는 (*n.* suspense 불안, 긴장)   vibrate 진동하다   decrease 감소하다 (↔ increase 증가하다)   heart rate 심박동 수   excitement 흥분   nervousness 불안   compression 압축 (*v.* compress 압축하다)   chest 가슴   pressure 압력

Several government studies have reported that the number of ① <u>overweight</u> children (double) since the 1970s and that 13 to 15 percent of children are now overweight. The studies mentioned a number of causes for this ② <u>increase</u>; however, the biggest factor is simply overeating. The average serving at the leading fast-food restaurants has ballooned with the ③ <u>avoidance</u> of "supersize" meals. Many busy families now eat at these restaurants several times a week because the service is ④ <u>fast</u>. *But careless consumers — including children — are paying a severe price in terms of their health, for they face a ⑤ <u>higher</u> risk of diabetes, heart disease, and other conditions.

1 윗글의 밑줄 친 부분 중, 문맥상 낱말의 쓰임이 적절하지 <u>않은</u> 것은?

①   ②   ③   ④   ⑤

서술형

2 괄호 안의 동사 double을 알맞은 형태로 쓰시오.

_____

Grammar Points!   접속사 for

for가 접속사로 사용될 경우 '왜냐하면'이라는 뜻의 이유를 나타낸다.
But careless consumers — including children — are paying a severe price in terms of their health, **for** they face a higher risk of diabetes, heart disease, and other conditions.
하지만 어린이들을 포함하여 부주의한 소비자들은 건강에 관한 한 혹독한 대가를 치르고 있는데, 왜냐하면 그들은 당뇨병, 심장병, 그리고 다른 질병들의 더 높은 위험에 직면하기 때문이다.

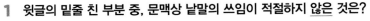

---

mention 언급하다   **cause** 원인 (↔ effect 결과)   **factor** 요인   **overeating** 과식   **balloon** (갑자기) 많아지다, 부풀다; 풍선   **avoidance** 기피 (v. avoid 피하다)   **consumer** 소비자 (v. consume 소비하다)   **severe** 혹독한, 심한   **in terms of** ~의 점에서   **face** 직면하다   **risk** 위험   **diabetes** 당뇨병

Your memory can play ① <u>tricks</u> on you. <u>It</u>'s often easy to forget things when you want desperately to remember them. You have probably had the experience of ② <u>forgetting</u> an acquaintance's name, which comes to mind only when it's too late. Perhaps you have also probably been ③ <u>unable</u> to find your keys because you put them down somewhere without thinking. At other times, however, *you may find it difficult to ④ <u>remember</u> some things even though you wish you could never think of them again. Some scholars believe that these ⑤ <u>annoying</u> habits of memory evolved for a reason. It's hard to imagine, though, any good reason for developing the ability to forget where you left your keys.

1 윗글의 밑줄 친 부분 중, 문맥상 낱말의 쓰임이 적절하지 <u>않은</u> 것은?

①   ②   ③   ④   ⑤

서술형
2 밑줄 친 It이 가리키는 내용을 우리말로 쓰시오.

_____

Grammar Points!   가목적어 it, 진목적어 to부정사 구문

『주어 + 동사 + 목적어 + 보어』의 5형식 문장에서 목적어가 to부정사구인 경우 가목적어 it을 쓰고 진목적어인 to부정사구는 뒤로 보낸다.
<u>You may find it difficult to remember some things.</u>
  S   V   가목적어 보어   진목적어
당신이 어떤 것들을 기억하는 게 어렵다는 것을 알게 될지도 모른다.

play a trick on ~에게 장난하다, 속이다   **desperately** 필사적으로   **experience** 경험   **acquaintance** 아는 사람   **come to mind** 기억나다   **scholar** 학자   **annoy** 괴롭히다   **evolve** 진화하다, 발전하다

(A)

The Sochi 2014 Winter Olympics was the longest in the 90-year history of the games. That's because the International Olympics Committee decided to add twelve new events. This does not mean, however, that future Winter Olympics will be as long.

(B)

Unfortunately, *even that did not seem to excite the viewers, and after 1992, it disappeared forever. By 2000, even the International Ski Federation decided that ski ballet was not "sport worthy" enough, marking the (a) death / birth of this graceful, but strange competition.

(C)

There are a few sports that made a grand debut and even lasted a few games, before being (b) presented / removed in favor of more exciting and popular sports. Ski ballet is one example. It involves gracefully performing jumps, flips and spins while skiing down a small hill.

(D)

The International Ski Federation first accepted the sport as a competitive freestyle skiing event in the 1960s. In 1988, the IOC considered adding it to the official events as a (c) competitive / demonstration sport. This meant that participants did not get medals.

1 주어진 글 (A)에 이어질 내용을 순서에 맞게 배열한 것으로 가장 적절한 것은?

① (B) − (C) − (D) ② (B) − (D) − (C) ③ (C) − (D) − (B)
④ (C) − (B) − (D) ⑤ (D) − (C) − (B)

2 (a), (b), (c)의 각 네모 안에서 문맥에 맞는 낱말로 가장 적절한 것은?

(a)	(b)	(c)
① death	removed	demonstration
② death	removed	competitive
③ birth	presented	demonstration
④ birth	presented	competitive
⑤ death	presented	demonstration

3 윗글의 ski ballet에 관한 내용과 일치하지 <u>않는</u> 것은?

① 2000년에 스포츠 종목에서 완전히 사라졌다.
② 올림픽에서 한 번도 경쟁 종목이었던 적이 없다.
③ 관람자들의 흥미를 끌지 못해서 올림픽에서 퇴출당한 종목이다.
④ 실외경기로서 점프, 플립, 스핀 등의 동작을 선보였다.
⑤ 1960년대에 국제스키연맹에 의해 올림픽의 시범 종목이 되었다.

서술형

4 밑줄 친 this graceful, but strange competition이 가리키는 것을 윗글에서 찾아 쓰시오.

_____

Grammar Points! 감정을 나타내는 동사

사람의 감정을 나타내는 동사는 대개 원형의 의미가 '~한 기분이 되게 만들다'의 뜻을 갖는다.
excite: 신나게 만들다 / exciting: 신나게 해주는 / excited: 신이 난
Even that did not seem to **excite** the viewers, and after 1992, it disappeared forever.
이마저도 관람자들의 흥미를 끌지 못한 것 같아서 1992년 이후에 그것은 영원히 사라졌다.

committee 위원회 event 사건, 종목 unfortunately 불행하게도 (↔ fortunately 다행스럽게) disappear 사라지다 (↔ appear 나타나다) federation 연맹, 연합 worthy 가치 있는 competition 시합, 경쟁 debut 첫 무대, 데뷔 remove 제거하다 in favor of ~ 편을 들어, ~을 위해 involve 포함하다 perform 공연하다, 수행하다 flip 플립, 갑자기 확 움직이기 spin 회전 demonstration 시범 participant 참가자

Word Check ✕ ✕ ✕

정답 및 해설 p.25

[1-10] 영어는 우리말로, 우리말은 영어로 나타내시오.

1 vibrate : _____

2 mention : _____

3 conscious : _____

4 involve : _____

5 remove : _____

6 경쟁의 : _____

7 아는 사람 : _____

8 고정시키다, 수리하다 : _____

9 드러내다, 폭로하다 : _____

10 위원회 : _____

[11-13] 괄호 안에서 알맞은 말을 고르시오.

11 Her family is (comprised / consisted) of two sons and a daughter.

12 In (favor / terms) of your proposal, don't you think you're asking for too much?

13 He bought (components / composition) for the television set he was repairing.

[14-16] 빈칸에 들어갈 말을 〈보기〉에서 골라 알맞은 형태로 쓰시오.

〈보기〉 perform   barrier   mimic

14 Duties and taxes are _____ to free trade.

15 Don't try to _____ anybody. Just be yourself.

16 Each part of the engine _____ a different function.

[17-18] 짝지어진 단어의 관계가 같도록 빈칸에 알맞은 말을 쓰시오.

17 increase : decrease = reject : _____

18 cause : effect = producer : _____

[19-21] 다음의 뜻에 해당하는 단어를 〈보기〉에서 골라 쓰시오.

〈보기〉 demonstration   evolve   desperately

19 _____ : to develop or achieve gradually

20 _____ : the act of showing or making evident, an explanation

21 _____ : in a way that seems like having lost all hope, extremely intense

Unit
16

문법성 판단

✖ 유형 소개

1. 밑줄 친 부분 중 어법상 틀린 것을 고르거나 어법에 맞는 표현을 고르는 형태로 출제된다.
2. 단순한 문법 지식을 묻는 문제와 글의 맥락을 통해서 문법의 적용 능력을 평가하는 문제가 모두 출제된다.
3. 자주 출제되는 문법 사항의 핵심 내용을 잘 숙지하고 문제를 많이 풀어보아야 한다.

✖ 유형 전략

Step 1 동사의 수, 시제, 태가 올바른지 점검한다. 특히 주어가 수식어구(형용사구, 전치사구, 분사구, 관계사절 등)로 인해 동사와 떨어져 있는 경우 동사의 수 일치에 유의한다.

Step 2 부정사, 동명사, 분사의 형태와 쓰임을 점검한다. 특히 목적격 보어로 쓰인 부정사와 분사에 주의하고 현재분사와 과거분사를 제대로 구분하여 썼는지 확인한다.

Step 3 관계사와 접속사의 의미와 형태가 올바른지 확인한다. 관계사와 선행사가 멀리 떨어진 경우, 선행사를 포함하고 있는 관계사 what에 특히 주의한다.

Step 4 가정법과 조동사의 의미와 형태에 주의하고 병렬구조에 맞는지, 어순이 올바른지 확인한다.

Words & Phrases

alien 외계의
appreciate 감지하다, 식별하다
beneath ~의 아래에
break 휴식, 휴지 기간
catch up with ~을 따라잡다
cautious 조심스러운
complete 완성하다, 완수하다
consequently 결과적으로
cut off 단절시키다, 잘라 내다
despite ~에도 불구하고
destroy 파괴하다
employment 고용, 직업
feature 특징, 자질
impress 감명을 주다

include 포함하다
laboratory 실험실
locate 두다, 위치를 정하다
manage 관리하다
opposite 정반대의
peer 동료, 또래
proportion 비율
scream 비명을 지르다, 소리치다
stuff 재료, 물자
trust 믿다, 신뢰하다
unfit 부적합한
uninteresting 흥미 없는, 지루한
yell 소리 지르다

Example

다음 글의 밑줄 친 부분 중 어법상 틀린 것은?

Washing hands with soap and water is the best way ① <u>to get</u> rid of germs. If soap and water are not available, use an alcohol-based hand sanitizer that contains at least 60% alcohol. You can tell ② <u>if</u> the sanitizer contains at least 60% alcohol by looking at the product label. Alcohol-based hand sanitizers can quickly reduce the number of germs on hands in some situations, but sanitizers do NOT get rid of all types of germs. Hand sanitizers may not be effective ③ <u>when</u> hands are visibly dirty or greasy. Furthermore, hand sanitizers might not remove harmful chemicals like pesticides and heavy metals from hands. Be cautious when ④ <u>used</u> sanitizers around children; ⑤ <u>swallowing</u> alcohol-based hand sanitizers can cause alcohol poisoning if a person swallows more than a couple mouthfuls.

✕ 문제 해결하기

Step 1 **기본적인 영문법 지식 갖추기**
기본적으로 많이 나오는 영문법 지식 없이 어법성 판단 문제를 풀 수 없다. 영어로 된 책에 많이 노출이 되던지 아니면 영문법 지식을 습득하는 것이 우선이다.

Step 2 **밑줄이 쳐진 문제의 경우 밑줄 부분에만 집중하라. 그래야 시간을 절약할 수 있다.**
① to부정사의 형용사적 용법으로 앞에 명사인 the best way를 수식한다. ② tell if+S+V~(~인지 알 수 있다) ③ '때'를 나타내는 종속접속사 ⑤ 동명사 주어 자리

Step 3 **정답 확인하기**
④ '접속사+분사' 문제로 use 뒤에 목적어가 있는 것으로 보아 현재분사인 using이 되어야 한다. 보통 과거 분사인 used 뒤에는 부사구(전치사구)가 나오지 목적어(명사)가 나오지 않는다. 'when (you are) using sanitizers around children'이라는 문장이 되어야 한다.

get rid of ~을 제거하다(= remove) germ 병균, 세균 available 이용 가능한 alcohol-based 알코올이 들어간 sanitizer 소독제, 세정제 contain 포함하다 at least 적어도 label 라벨, 딱지, 상표 greasy 기름에 전, 기름기 많은 harmful 해로운 pesticide 농약 cautious 조심스러운 swallow 꿀꺽 삼키다; 제비 mouthful 한 모금

Lake Vida isn't like other lakes. For one thing, it's in Antarctica. For another, it's located deep beneath a 60-foot-thick slab of ice, and has consequently ① <u>cut</u> off from the surface world for 2,800 years ② <u>untouched</u> by outside oxygen or light. *The water in Lake Vida is acidic, starved of oxygen, and so salty ③ <u>that</u> it remains liquid despite its temperature ④ <u>hovering</u> around the -13°C mark all year round. Now after years of drilling, scientists have discovered samples of previously unknown species of bacteria swimming around in it, ⑤ <u>suggesting</u> that life can exist in conditions previously deemed unfit. The discovery of the ecosystem may inform the search for alien microbes on other planets, such as Mars, or on icy moons such as Jupiter's Europa.

1 윗글의 밑줄 친 부분 중 어법상 <u>틀린</u> 것은?

①   ②   ③   ④   ⑤

서술형

2 윗글에서 과학자들이 Lake Vida에서 발견한 것은 무엇이며 그것이 시사하는 바를 찾아 우리말로 쓰시오.

Grammar Points! 제거, 분리, 박탈의 전치사 of

전치사 of를 동반하여 제거, 분리, 박탈의 의미를 나타내는 말에는 starve A of B (A에게서 B를 빼앗다) / deprive A of B (A에게서 B를 빼앗다) / rob A of B (A에게서 B를 강탈하다) / relieve A of B (A에게서 B를 경감하다) / clear A of B (A에서 B를 치우다) 등이 있다.

The water in Lake Vida is acidic, **starved of** oxygen, and so salty that it remains liquid despite its temperature hovering around the -13°C mark all year round. Vida호의 물은 산소를 빼앗겨 산성이며 염분이 매우 높아서 온도가 일 년 내내 영하 13도 언저리를 유지함에도 불구하고 액체로 머물러 있다.

Antarctica 남극 대륙   locate 두다. 위치를 정하다   beneath ∼의 아래에   slab 납작한 조각   consequently 결과적으로   cut off 단절시키다. 잘라 내다
acidic 산성의 (n. acid 산)   starve A of B A에게서 B를 빼앗다(주로 수동태로 쓰임)   despite ∼에도 불구하고   hover 맴돌다   previously 이전에
deem ∼으로 생각하다   unfit 부적합한   alien 외계의   microbe 세균. 미생물   Jupiter 목성   Europa 유로파(목성의 위성)

You (A) [may / should] have heard of strange stuff called antimatter in science fiction movies — but it is actually science fact. Every type of matter particle has a mirror image, or antiparticle. For instance, the electron's antiparticle is the positron. It has the same mass but opposite features, such as charge. If a particle hits its antiparticle, they are both destroyed in a burst of energy. Particles and antiparticles are created and (B) [destroy / destroyed] all the time in cosmic rays, which bombard Earth from space. Scientists can make microscopic amounts of antimatter in the laboratory. They hope to make enough (C) [power / to power] a spacecraft; *just a teaspoonful could send a rocket to Mars.

* electron 전자, 일렉트론   * positron 양전자

---

1 (A), (B), (C)의 각 네모 안에서 어법에 맞는 표현으로 가장 적절한 것은?

	(A)	(B)	(C)
①	may	destroy	power
②	may	destroy	to power
③	may	destroyed	to power
④	should	destroy	power
⑤	should	destroyed	to power

서술형

2 What happens when a particle hits its antiparticle? Answer in Korean.

_____

Grammar Points!   **명사 주어가 if절을 대신하는 경우**

가정법 조건절의 의미가 명사 주어에 내포되어 있는 경우가 있다. 이 경우 동사의 형태를 통해 가정법 조건절이 주어에 포함되어 있음을 알 수 있으며, 명사 주어를 조건절로 고쳐 쓸 수 있다.

Just a teaspoonful could send a rocket to Mars. 찻숟가락 하나의 양으로도 로켓을 화성까지 보낼 수 있을 것이다.
= If they made just a teaspoonful (of antimatter), it could send ~.

---

stuff 재료, 물자   **antimatter** 반물질 (접두사 anti- 반대의)   **particle** 분자, 미립자   **mass** 질량   **opposite** 정반대의   **feature** 특징, 자질   **charge** 전하(물체가 띠고 있는 정전기)   **destroy** 파괴하다   **burst** 파열, 폭발   **cosmic** 우주의 (*n.* cosmos 우주)   **bombard** 포격하다, 퍼붓다 (*n.* bomb 폭탄)   **microscopic** 현미경의, 극히 작은 (*n.* microscope 현미경)   **laboratory** 실험실   **teaspoonful** 찻숟가락 하나의 양, 소량

Over winter break I finally decided to read the copy of the book that (A) ⎡is / had been⎤ sitting in my room for years. It was a long endeavor (B) ⎡while / since⎤ my copy had around 1,400 pages, but I did it. Although the section on the Bishop and the sections of French history were often uninteresting, I was impressed overall with the amount of detail that the novel included. *There's so much more to be known about each of the characters, and I really appreciate the nuances the book (C) ⎡conveying / conveys⎤ that the musical or movie adaptations simply had no time to include. Some things, like Javert's fixation on Valjean, still never became clear to me, but other things, like Cosette's relationship with Marius, made sense with context.

1 (A), (B), (C)의 각 네모 안에서 어법에 맞는 표현으로 가장 적절한 것은?

(A)		(B)		(C)
① is	······	while	······	conveying
② is	······	since	······	conveys
③ had been	······	while	······	conveying
④ had been	······	since	······	conveys
⑤ had been	······	since	······	conveying

서술형
2 윗글에서 필자가 읽은 책에서 필자가 가장 인상 깊게 생각한 특징 하나를 찾아 쓰시오.

_____

Grammar Points!　부정사의 수동태

부정사의 수동태는 『to be p.p.』의 형태로 나타낸다.
There's so much more **to be known** about each of the characters.
각 등장인물에 대해서는 훨씬 더 많은 것을 알아야만 한다.

break 휴식, 휴지 기간　endeavor 노력, 시도　uninteresting 흥미 없는, 지루한　impress 감명을 주다　overall 전체적으로　detail 세부 사항　include 포함하다　appreciate 감지하다, 식별하다　nuance 뉘앙스, 미묘한 차이　convey 전하다, 시사하다　adaptation 개작물, 각색 (v. adapt 개작하다)　fixation 고착, 애착 (v. fix 고정시키다)　make sense 의미가 통하다　context 문맥, 맥락

"Mom, why don't you ever take me out to dinner?" Ginger screamed. "All my friends go out to dinner at (A) least / most once a week. They go to nice restaurants and they have a good time. They make me sick!" Emily replied, "How many times (B) I have told / have I told you that I don't trust restaurant food? All you have to do is watch those specials on TV news programs to see (C) that / what is going on in the kitchen. When you see how the cooks don't wash after using the bathroom, how they sweat into your food while it's cooking, and how they touch every bite of your food with their hands, then you'd agree with me." "You exaggerate," Ginger yelled. *"Not all restaurants are like that — only a few!" Emily told her daughter that even a few was one too many for her.

1 (A), (B), (C)의 각 네모 안에서 어법에 맞는 표현으로 가장 적절한 것은?

	(A)	(B)	(C)
①	least	I have told	that
②	least	have I told	what
③	least	have I told	that
④	most	I have told	that
⑤	most	have I told	what

서술형

2 Emily가 Ginger를 식당에 데려가지 않는 이유를 20자 이내의 우리말로 쓰시오.

_____

Grammar Points!   수량 형용사 few

셀 수 있는 명사에 대해 수의 정도를 나타내는 few의 용법은 다음과 같다.
a few (약간의) / few (거의 없는) / not a few (꽤 많은) / only[but] a few (아주 적은, 거의 없는)
Not all restaurants are like that — only a few! 모든 식당이 그런 것은 아니에요. 아주 일부란 말이에요!
cf. 셀 수 없는 명사를 꾸며줄 때는 few 대신 little을 사용하여 a little, little, not a little(적지 않게, 크게) 등으로 나타낸다.

scream 비명을 지르다, 소리치다   once a week 일주일에 한 번   sick 속이 메스꺼운, 울화가 치미는   trust 믿다, 신뢰하다   sweat 땀을 흘리다   bite 소량의 음식, 한 입   exaggerate 과장하다   yell 소리 지르다   only a few 다만 몇 안 되는

NEETs are young people (A) ⬚age / aged⬚ between 15 and 29 years old who are not in employment, education or training. *The proportion of young people neither working nor studying can be used when we explain how well economies manage the transition between school and work. In fact, it gives information about those not in education, which youth unemployment rates (B) ⬚do / does⬚ not take into account. It's especially illuminating when the figures are broken down into those who are still looking for work ("unemployed") and those who have dropped out of the labor market altogether ("inactive"). Particularly worrying (C) ⬚is / are⬚ those in the very youngest age bracket – aged 15 to 19 – who may not have completed their secondary education and are even likely not to be seeking work. There's a risk they may never catch up with their better-educated peers.

1 (A), (B), (C)의 각 네모 안에서 어법에 맞는 표현으로 가장 적절한 것은?

	(A)	(B)	(C)
①	age	do	is
②	age	does	are
③	aged	do	is
④	aged	do	are
⑤	aged	does	are

[서술형]

2 윗글에 의하면 NEETs와 청년실업률은 어떤 차이가 있는지 우리말로 쓰시오.

_____

Grammar Points! neither A nor B

'A도 아니고 B도 아닌'이라는 양자 부정의 의미이다. A와 B는 문법상 같은 형태이어야 함에 주의한다.
The proportion of young people **neither** working **nor** studying can be used when we explain how well economies manage the transition between school and work.
일을 하지도 않고 공부를 하지도 않는 젊은이의 비율은 경제 상태가 학교에서 직장으로의 이동을 얼마나 잘 관리하고 있는지를 설명할 때 사용될 수 있다.

employment 고용, 직업 proportion 비율 manage 관리하다 transition 이행, 이동 unemployment rate 실업률 take into account 고려하다 (= consider) illuminating 조명하는, 밝히는 figure 수치 break down (분석할 수 있도록) 나누다 drop out of ~에서 떨어져 나가다 labor market 노동 시장 bracket 부류, 괄호 complete 완성하다, 완수하다 catch up with ~을 따라잡다 peer 동료, 또래

Word Check ✕ ✕ ✕

정답 및 해설 p.27

[1-10] 영어는 우리말로, 우리말은 영어로 나타내시오.

1   beneath : _____

2   particle : _____

3   transition : _____

4   employment : _____

5   endeavor : _____

6   등장인물 : _____

7   표면 : _____

8   세균, 미생물 : _____

9   과장하다 : _____

10   동료, 또래 : _____

[11-13] 괄호 안에서 알맞은 말을 고르시오.

11   The author uses metaphors to (convey / survey) his thoughts.

12   We didn't fully (appreciate / appropriate) that he was seriously ill.

13   She has just (competed / completed) a master's degree in Law.

[14-16] 빈칸에 들어갈 말을 〈보기〉에서 골라 알맞은 형태로 쓰시오.

〈보기〉 catch   cut   starve

14   I was scared that one day my past problems would _____ up with me.

15   He _____ himself off from all human contact.

16   The project is being _____ of funds.

[17-18] 짝지어진 단어의 관계가 같도록 빈칸에 알맞은 말을 쓰시오.

17   active : inactive = fit : _____

18   cosmos : cosmic = acid : _____

[19-21] 다음의 뜻에 해당하는 단어를 〈보기〉에서 골라 쓰시오.

〈보기〉 adaptation   fixation   particle

19   _____ : the act of changing something to make it suitable for a new purpose

20   _____ : a very small piece or amount of something, a piece of matter smaller than an atom

21   _____ : thinking about a particular subject or person to an excessive degree

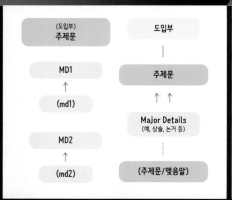

① 구문
판매 1위 '천일문' 콘텐츠를 활용하여 정확하고 다양한 구문 학습

(끊어읽기) (해석하기) (문장 구조 분석) (해설·해석 제공) (단어 스크램블링) (영작하기)

② 문법·서술형
쎄듀의 모든 문법 문항을 활용하여 내신까지 해결하는 정교한 문법 유형 제공

(객관식과 주관식의 결합) (문법 포인트별 학습) (보기를 활용한 집합 문항) (내신대비 서술형) (어법+서술형 문제)

③ 어휘
초·중·고·공무원까지 방대한 어휘량을 제공하며 오프라인 TEST 인쇄도 가능

(영단어 카드 학습) (단어 ↔ 뜻 유형) (예문 활용 유형) (단어 매칭 게임)

④ 선생님 보유 문항 이용

(Online Test) (OMR Test)

공든탑이 무너지랴!

첫단추 BASIC 시리즈

중학부터 세우는 **튼튼한 수능 영어의 탑**

첫단추 BASIC
문법·어법편 1, 2

1 수능 영어에 꼭 필요한
핵심 문법·어법 엄선

2 다양한 유형의 문제로
문법 적용력 향상

첫단추 BASIC
독해편 1, 2

1 글에 대한 기본 개념부터
문제 유형별 이해까지 완성

2 실전 맛보기용 미니 모의고사
각 권당 4회분 수록

후속 교재

수능 영어 실전 정복의 첫걸음
첫단추 시리즈

독해유형편 / 독해실전편 / 문법·어법편 / 듣기유형편 / 듣기실전편

쎄듀

1센치 영문법

쉽고 빠르게 한 달 안에 끝!

1센치 영문법

1cm English Grammar

- 1cm의 책 두께로 중등과 고등 영어의 틈을 메운다!
- 1회 완독으로 영문법이 한눈에 들어온다!
- 1권으로 꼭 알아야 할 핵심만 담았다!
- 1페이지 개념 정리로 쉽고 빠르게 넘겨간다!

김기훈
인지영
강민진
강민지

CEDU BOOK 쎄듀

한 달 안에 끝!
영어 문법과 더 가까워지는 지름길!

01 기초 영문법의 결정판!

02 각종 커뮤니티에 올라온 수많은 영문법 질문을 분석!

03 학생들이 어려워하는 영문법의 핵심을 쉽게 빠르게 정리!

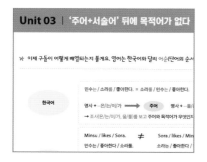

Warming Up!

어떤 개념을 배울지 그림으로 미리 보기!
도형으로 핵심 문법을 빠르게 파악!

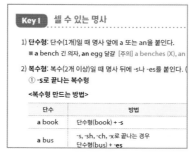

Key Points!

핵심 문법만 쉽고 간단하게!

실력 Up!

단계별 문제로 핵심 문법 익히기!
다양한 문제로 영문법 기초를 튼튼하게!

쎄듀 초등 커리큘럼

	예비초	초1	초2	초3	초4	초5	초6
구문		신간 천일문 365 일력	초1-3	초등코치 천일문 SENTENCE			
		교육부 지정 초등 필수 영어 문장		1001개 문장 암기로 완성하는 초등 영어의 기초			
문법				초등코치 천일문 GRAMMAR			
				1001개 예문으로 배우는 초등 영문법			
		신간 왓츠 Grammar Start 시리즈					
		초등 기초 영문법 입문					
					신간 왓츠 Grammar Plus 시리즈		
					초등 필수 영문법 마무리		
독해				신간 왓츠 리딩 70 / 80 / 90 / 100 A / B			
				쉽고 재미있게 완성되는 영어 독해력			
어휘				초등코치 천일문 VOCA&STORY			
				1001개의 초등 필수 어휘와 짧은 스토리			
		패턴으로 말하는 초등 필수 영단어 1 / 2		문장 패턴으로 완성하는 초등 필수 영단어			
ELT	Oh! My PHONICS 1 / 2 / 3 / 4						
	유·초등학생을 위한 첫 영어 파닉스						
		Oh! My SPEAKING 1 / 2 / 3 / 4 / 5 / 6					
		핵심 문장 패턴으로 더욱 쉬운 영어 말하기					
		Oh! My GRAMMAR 1 / 2 / 3		쓰기로 완성하는 첫 초등 영문법			

쎄듀 중등 커리큘럼

	예비중	중1	중2	중3
구문		신간 천일문 STARTER 1 / 2		중등 필수 구문 & 문법 총정리
문법		천일문 GRAMMAR LEVEL 1 / 2 / 3		예문 중심 문법 기본서
		GRAMMAR Q Starter 1, 2 / Intermediate 1, 2 / Advanced 1, 2		학기별 문법 기본서
		잘 풀리는 영문법 1 / 2 / 3		문제 중심 문법 적용서
		GRAMMAR PIC 1 / 2 / 3 / 4		이해가 쉬운 도식화된 문법서
			1센치 영문법	1권으로 핵심 문법 정리
문법+어법			첫단추 BASIC 문법·어법편 1 / 2	문법·어법의 기초
문법+쓰기	EGU 영단어&품사 / 문장 형식 / 동사 써먹기 / 문법 써먹기 / 구문 써먹기			서술형 기초 세우기와 문법 다지기
				올씀 1 기본 문장 PATTERN
				내신 서술형 기본 문장 학습
쓰기		거침없이 Writing LEVEL 1 / 2 / 3		중등 교과서 내신 기출 서술형
		개정 중학 영어 쓰작 1 / 2 / 3		중등 교과서 패턴 드릴 서술형
어휘		어휘끝 중학 필수편	중학 필수어휘 1000개	어휘끝 중학 마스터편
				고난도 중학어휘 +고등기초 어휘 1000개
독해		Reading Relay Starter 1, 2 / Challenger 1, 2 / Master 1, 2		타교과 연계 배경 지식 독해
		READING Q Starter 1, 2 / Intermediate 1, 2 / Advanced 1, 2		예측/추론/요약 사고력 독해
독해전략			리딩 플랫폼 1 / 2 / 3	논픽션 지문 독해
독해유형			Reading 16 LEVEL 1 / 2 / 3	수능 유형 맛보기 + 내신 대비
			첫단추 BASIC 독해편 1 / 2	수능 유형 독해 입문
듣기	Listening Q 유형편 / 1 / 2 / 3			유형별 듣기 전략 및 실전 대비
		쎄듀 빠르게 중학영어듣기 모의고사 1 / 2 / 3		교육청 듣기평가 대비

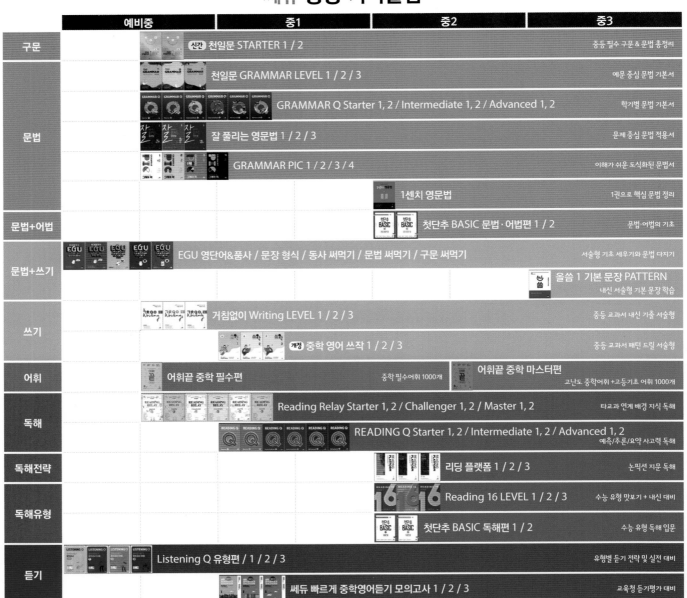